COLLAGE OF LIFE

*When mere seconds change the course
of you life inside the hospitals and those
that work behind the scenes.*

CERA GRACE

Copyright © 2016 by Cera Grace

Collage Of Life
When mere seconds change the course of you life inside the hospitals and those that work behind the scenes.

by Cera Grace

Printed in the United States of America.

Edited by Xulon Press.

ISBN 9781498461337

All rights reserved solely by the author. The author guarantees all contents are original and do not infringe upon the legal rights of any other person or work. No part of this book may be reproduced in any form without the permission of the author. The views expressed in this book are not necessarily those of the publisher.

Unless otherwise indicated, Scripture quotations taken from the King James Version (KJV) – *public domain.*

www.xulonpress.com

Table of Contents

Introduction vii
Collage of Life: Overview ix

Chapter 1	Colors of Yellow 13
Chapter 2	Consequences of Youth 17
Chapter 3	Crumbs of Life 22
Chapter 4	Friday Night Lights 25
Chapter 5	Close to Home 29
Chapter 6	Last Flight of Hope 34
Chapter 7	Lifetime Love 40
Chapter 8	Never Give Up 43
Chapter 9	No Answers to Some Whys 46
Chapter 10	Power of Words 50
Chapter 11	The Green Mile 56
Chapter 12	The Little Red Hen 61
Chapter 13	Time 65
Chapter 14	Locked In 67
Chapter 15	We Can't Take You 70
Chapter 16	Lonely 74
Chapter 17	Mere Seconds 76
Chapter 18	Artificial Lights 78
Chapter 19	Aha Moments 82
Chapter 20	Acknowledging the Unworthy 85
Chapter 21	The Gift of Life 87

Mom's Letter from Heaven: Dedication 91

Introduction: Collage Book

When we are new with the Holy Spirit and learning God's grace during adversities in life, we seek answers, and I often reflect on Psalms 42:1. "As a deer pants for water so shall we thirst for thee." I smile thinking of the day that I learned that scripture. Today as I seek answers and ask God for direction, a deer appears before me. I often smile and with gladness as I recall that moment.

I was working down on the coast in Biloxi and returning from a turbulent time in my life. I was running, yet staying close to home, which is still six hours away. Anywhere within the state of Mississippi or Alabama, I found solace.

I was driving home and I felt so lost; my spirit was broken, and I had gotten to a point in my life where I was dealing with so many things. My mother-in-law had died a few months previously. I was seeking answers and was ridden with guilt. The inevitable divorce was about to begin its course in my life. It had been coming for many years because I felt that he didn't love me, and by him not seek counseling, I felt so unworthy. Never should I have placed such a weight on this kind man. I shall always take my own accountability for not seeing my own self-worth. Physically and emotionally I was dying inside. He was too, but neither knew how to help the other.

It is about to become dusk, and the sky was this earth-tone of vermillion as the sunset colors coated the sky. I spoke to God as if he was a passenger in the car. I was crying and felt such despair. As I looked to the right, this huge deer with large antlers looked right into my soul, or so I felt. I rushed to pull over, and as I stopped, I noticed a lake beyond to the right. I reached for my phone and searched for deer in the Bible, and this scripture leapt out as if God had spoken it directly to me. Looking back, I know that he did. This deer was seeking water as I was seeking God. I smiled and each burden that I felt was lifted. I drove into the night to the place I called home, even though I didn't do much living there over the years.

I am reminded that during that trip, those few weeks on the coast, my son had called me crying a few nights earlier. He had told me that he had been saved. He said, "Mom, I got saved today and I wanted to call you because I knew that you would understand." He felt he didn't deserve this gift of peace, yet I knew my son would forever be in God's hands. It is a moment in life that you never forget.

I am now divorced and seeing this man who has pulled me through so much. A winter storm is coming in, which in the south is like a free unpaid holiday for the state to enjoy. He had asked me to stay the night on the couch in case the weather was bad the next day. He made so many trips downstairs to make sure that I was ok that eventually, I just got up to come home. At dinner I had told him that I had seen five deer from my patio prior to coming over. He doesn't share or understand my enthusiasm for them.

I leave, and as I am turning into my quaint little home, five deer are in the road. They hear the gravel as the tires pass and look for the source of the noise! I smiled because I knew that I was home. I was safe inside with faith inconceivable to most. Home is not a structure. Home is where you feel safe inside yourself.

God bless, Cera

Collage Of Life: Overview

Many of us have been stuck in life with no ability to move forward. We have lost hope and are often left just living life to the best of our abilities. For years I told people stories about the things that I saw working as a nurse, and each one would say, "You ought to write a book." Most of the time, I shrugged it off, keeping it in the back of my mind.

As a child I wanted to be a famous singer. I wanted to be an actress; I wanted to sip sherry as they did on the soap operas that my grandmother often watched. I wanted to wear the silks and pastels portrayed in the movies; I wanted to marry my prince charming; and I wanted life to be like the fairy tales.

Let me just say, that did not work. God has humor because these were unrealistic dreams; they were fantasies that I used to escape as a child. For some reason I was granted a greater life than I had expected.

I did not become that famous singer, but often I sing on karaoke nights with my sisters. I have been blessed to be an actress, reading the script of a chart and finding someone's story. I did sip sherry, which I only had to do once. I do have the silks and pastels—maybe not the runway versions but the knock-offs that still make me feel like I am in a movie. I married a good man, yet later divorced, maybe because it wasn't "the dream." My dream was to be loved and cherished. Sadly, like all soap operas of life, it just doesn't work, and my fairy tales never became realities.

I ended up going to nursing school to be a Pharmaceutical Sales rep, yet I had to settle for being a registered nurse (RN). It is from these stories in the emergency room (ER), Intensive Care Unit (ICU), and Critical Care Units of life, that I had kept hidden inside my thoughts, buried in the whole of my soul, that I came to understand that God's purpose for my life was to show others the impact that life brings to each of us.

These stories are important to read, and it is important to understand their depth. I heard once that you can't believe there is a God without knowing that there is a Satan, meaning there is always good and bad in the world.

These stories are not sad or dark to me. It's how society and people label and judge others. They are of events that passed before my eyes in life. These are true stories: they actually happened. All the names are fictitious because of privacy laws.

This book is about what goes on inside a hospital within the circles of life. It is how each person holds a meaning, both in my life and in the lives of others. I did not write these stories during the years that I was working. It was only when I went through a divorce and almost lost my own child that these stories, that were handprints on my heart, became visual, and I wrote them down. Nineteen years of stories surfaced in my words, and, even today, they remain in my collage of life.

I think nurses get little credit in life. We often are the sounding board for patients who are angry at doctors, and who don't have the courage to speak to someone of a higher status with such anger. We are the maids, the ones held accountable if a doctor misses something. We are the ones to see many inhale their last breath of life, and often we are the ones to see the signs necessary to prevent that from happening. I do not think nurses get the credit they deserve, but then again, this is why we are caring. This is why I have these stories to share, and to me, it is to show you how deeply that we care for mankind.

Doctors care as well. I just think their workloads are massive, as are those of nurses, and even more so now. I think we have good and bad nurses and doctors. I don't think that the bad ones mean to be; I think it comes from the coping mechanisms that they use to mentally deal with life and death every working day of their lives.

I was fortunate to have been in the transformation of nursing as it evolved. I got to travel and see the world on someone else's dime. I was blessed beyond anything that I could have imagined for my life.

We all have a story. The people listed in these stories only passed by my life briefly. They made a difference, and their lives mattered to me and to their loved ones. Never should we forget that we all have a story to share. Never take a day for granted. Pay it forward by not judging others, by being kind to others, and just by loving others. The only degree that takes is grace. Grace is earned through acceptance, knowledge, and the love of the one I call Father.

God bless, Cera

Chapter 1:

Colors of Yellow

I went through a phase in life of curiosity; I wanted to learn things that other people didn't. During one phase I was interested in colors. Yellow is the color of sunshine and warmth. It is the color of the rays that radiate to others. It is a great color to wear when the sun has bronzed your skin with its rays in the summertime.

On the flip side, it is used in descriptions by grandparents and elders to say, "He is a yellow coward." Its meaning depends on context and intent. It is a color that I have charted often and have seen in the skin tone of patients' whole bodies or the tint of the whites of their eyes. I recalled the first patient I saw whose whole body was the color best described as banana Laffy Taffy. There was an artificial color in its presence; it would be the natural color of the peel of a banana, only it belonged to an elderly woman. This was the first time I saw and felt death as a nurse.

I was a new grad on this medical surgery floor. Like all nurses new at this time, the fear of death always permeated the halls. When a patient dies, the work load increases for the nurses. Those who are caught up with rounds try to fall into place to help with the tasks of notifying the family, getting a doctor to pronounce the death, calling the coroner, charting before and after on the patient, and finding out which funeral home will be taking in the deceased. Seldom do many nurses pitch in because their own load is too great. This night when I heard of the death, I walked to the room where the paperwork process was beginning.

Now understand, death frightened me beyond any words, emotions, or comprehension I had at this stage in life. As I walked into the room, this color of yellow that was before me was shocking all by itself. Never had I seen such a color of yellow on the human body. Each cell, nerve fiber, and heartbeat this lady had previously had was the color yellow or so I thought.

I approached the bed, as close as my steps will let me go, and then I heard the door shut. I gasped, and this feeling penetrated every cell in my body. It seemed like I and everything around me froze. I was frightened; I couldn't move; I couldn't breathe; nor could I turn my body to run. My body was cold; the air that surrounded me was cold, and all I could do was look to the ceiling.

I remember movies where people died and their spirit was floating above. They were trying to talk and say, "I am not dead. See, I am awake." We all recall some movie that still reminds us of Hollywood's version of death back then. All I remember is that I wanted out of that room, away from this woman. I ran out of that room with speed even I didn't know I had. I can't explain it; I don't understand it to this day, but I did not like what I felt in that room.

I grant you that I could walk right into that room today and remember the color of yellow, the presence of fright, and I still could not explain it any more than I can right now.

I went to help the nurse and ask her what I could do. She asked me to call the family and see which funeral home they want her to go to, or I could help someone put her in a body bag and place the tag on her toe. There was no way I would ever step back into that room, and I was not touching the body. After those brief seconds inside, there was absolutely no way. So I chose to call the family, and then I would be done and back to my own patients. God has humor because for sure it still permeates my stories even today.

I got the chart, and I began to find the information. I called the family and found that this lady had no children. I knew nothing of her life, what got her here, or why she died that night. As the phone was answered, this harsh voice on the other end told me that she was Sue's niece.

I explained that Sue had died, and we needed to know which funeral home the family would like to use. Before I could finish, the woman on the other line asked, "Well, which one is the cheapest?"

I was in shock. Why would someone ask this? How do you answer this question? How do you even begin to acknowledge such disrespect of someone who had just died? It was not what I was accustomed to as a human being or as a niece. Do you think shock is a word? Well get a question like this, and all sense of professionalism wishes to leave your voice, but it can't, so you just do the best you can.

After a brief conversation about the funeral homes available in the area, I give her the numbers to call and asked her to call the nurse back with the information. As I hung up the phone, I explained to my friend Pam, who had this patient, what had transpired. I explained how infuriated I was with this family member, how shocked I was at her disrespect.

"You have no idea how this woman was in life. Was she kind to her family? Did she cause mass destruction in their lives, or what? You have no idea how this woman was. Girl, you just don't know, so you can't judge," Pam replied.

I had never actually thought of another side. Right, wrong, or indifferent, I just didn't know.

I can tell you, later in life I learned I had animosity for someone who had died. At the time I didn't see it, but I spewed venom at times as well. Looking back now I realize that none of us has the right to judge. We each should be kind, respectful, and always thankful in the end of our lives here.

Maybe we can be surrounded with love, family, and friends who celebrate our life. We would be aghast if anyone asked, "Which is the cheapest?" We get that choice. Isn't it wonderful to understand that we have the choice to be the best that we can be?

Sadly, to this day I wonder what this woman's pain was for so many years. Why was no one at her side when those cells of life turned yellow? Looking back on my life that could have been me. It could very well become of you. Be kind, be forgiving, and love all. God gave us one new commandment after Jesus died, and that was to love. If we keep the first and second commandments, as a friend pointed out to me today, the others wouldn't be broken. See, I broke it inside that room with fear; I broke it on the phone with the niece; and then I broke it by judging another.

Thank you, God, for giving me the way, the truth, and the light through your love. No matter what color my skin radiates with my last breath in life, I hope it is filled with tears of joy and love beyond any bad memory that I may have of anyone or any cruel things I have said prior to this understanding.

Chapter 2

Consequences of Youth

People will show up at the door of the ER, and we have no idea what is going on with them or what has happened to bring them speeding to our doors of safety. One Sunday night around midnight, I was close to those doors and saw this small, beat up truck approach. This truck fit into the background of the mountains because the region is poor, and like always, I watched the moments unfold.

This young man, about twenty-two, got out and began to yell. I don't know if my mother instinct took over since I have a son a few years younger, or if my nurse instinct surfaced. Being a mom and a nurse and working ER, you can just tell from the timbre of someone's voice that they are frightened. It's the same when you hear your child's cry. Just by the sound, you know if it is a cry you need to answer immediately or one to let pass. A mother knows the cry of hurt.

This young man ran into my arms and said, "You have to help my friend." I turned and called for everyone to help and began to hear the day's events as I ran to the truck. As I approached and opened the passenger door, I was greeted with the vision of a young man. He was faceless to the point that there was no visibility to even see his eyes. He stood up and collapsed into my arms. Now, I am of a small frame, and this young man, Jake, was around one hundred and eighty pounds and over six feet tall. I noticed the most beautiful locks of curly dark hair, soaked with what appeared to be streaks of blood. How I held this man is beyond me, but within a few seconds one of the paramedics took his weight and placed him on the gurney.

He was rushed to the trauma room, and I began to relay what was told to me. Jake had gotten up that morning and gone riding on his dirt bike alone. Based off the fragrance of his breath, a few cases of beer went along with him. This is not a great combination, but he was young and didn't understand the consequences. Jake decided to race his bike on the back roads of the Appalachian Mountains that day alone. In the process of this ride, his bike turned over at a great speed. Because he didn't have a helmet on, upon impact his face landed on the pavement and took the weight and speed of the crash. I am sure his face slid on the pavement for yards that day.

If you work in ER, most of the time after you wash away the blood and you see where the damage is, it isn't as bad as it looks. This, however, was not one of those times. As I wiped the blood away from his wounds, still all I could see was his curly hair. I thought sweetly of my son's hair and wondered if Jake had a mother. Jake was trying to talk but the words were inaudible. I placed my hand over his and explained that he shouldn't talk and should let me clean this area. I could tell he was in shock because he was calm; he had no clarity of the events. He was calmer than anyone I have ever seen who had experienced such trauma. Looking at his physical features, the skin tone, the texture of his arms and legs, and this beautiful head of hair, my guess was that Jake was around nineteen years old. My heart, just for a second, beat in the base of my throat and I continued to clean his face. Many others were in the room and helping, including the trauma doctor. Jake was stabilized, and we were trying to stop the blood, so we could fly him to a larger trauma hospital down the mountains.

Blood continued to flow from wounds we had yet to see, and the floor of the trauma room looked like Hollywood gore. I got to Jake's mouth, and I noticed the reason his words weren't audible; his tongue was sliced vertically. There was no skin to cover his face; his eyes were barely visible; and no color is noted because they were closed. If not they would be holding sockets for the blood flowing down his face. Jake had a huge gash in his head; his tongue was hanging by mere fibers; he had no more eyebrows; he had two fingers on his right hand that had no skin, only bones were protruding. When I touched his hand earlier, I didn't feel these bones. I assume this was a reflex his body used as a defensive mechanism and it also met pavement with this crash. Jake was faceless; his hands were stripped of the skin tissue and muscle, as was his chest. In the midst of observing all these features, I wondered how many plastic surgeries he would endure over his life as a consequence of his youthful mistake today.

During our observation, we received a call saying that the air evacuation would arrive in minutes, and we needed to have him ready to go. When someone is transferred like this, there is one nurse and a unit coordinator filling out the paperwork. He can't be transferred until the nurse calls the report in to the facility that accepts him. The MD has to find a physician to accept him as well. All this has to be documented along with the events. It is a critical documentation and transfer of accountability for all involved.

Everyone except me left the room. I explained to Jake what was about to happen. I told him everything would be ok, and soon he would be one of the cutest boys living on the Appalachian Mountains, but it would take some time. With those words his eyes opened because we had stopped some of the bleeding. I noticed a smile that lacked a few teeth at the moment, but it was one of the prettiest things I had seen that night. Judging by those locks of curls and the thickness of his hair, he was probably considered adorable by the girls his age.

Before Jake was flown out, and as we approached the helicopter, I said to him, "Jake never do drugs or drink again until you can make right choices. Tonight it only cost you a few fingers and the skin off your face, but next time it may be someone's life."

He replied with words that were barely audible. He said, "Yes ma'am," and I smiled because that was the same thing my son would have said.

I didn't understand how the events of that night would affect me until the next day. I was sitting outside, soaking in the briskness of the mountains, when I thought of Jake and my cell phone rang. My son, who was still young and attending a prominent college, attempted to speak. His words were not audible and he sounded like he was crying. He couldn't speak, and I asked "Son, what is wrong?" It took a few seconds for him to get the tears to stop and the words to come out. He said, "Mom, Taylor died last night." Taylor had been a friend for years. I had just seen Taylor at the last ballgame. He had been accepted into law school, and he was trying to get off drugs. Taylor was the oldest of three boys in his family. His younger brother had died around seven years ago at the age of fifteen in an automobile accident involving alcohol and drugs. When I last spoke to Taylor at the ballgame, I was introduced to his mom. I remember telling her how even thought I had just met her, that I often thought of her and the son she lost the previous years. She began to cry and reached out to hug me. She knew I thanked God that it wasn't my son, but I understood the depth of that fear; I just hadn't lived it.

As I listened to my son relay the story, he said Taylor had come in around midnight, gone to bed, and never woken up. He had overdosed on methadone and Xanax. I remembered last night's events in ER and the timing of Jake's arrival. I silently thanked God that Jake would live. I began to cry as my son spoke, and I thought of Taylor's mom and the fact she has now lost two of her three children. I think of the load that the only son left will have to endure. I weep for the risks so many take in their young adult years, and all I can do is pray.

After my son and I hung up, I called the hospital where Jake was transported, and I spoke with the nurse that was with him. I asked if his mother is there, and she replies, "Yes, just hold on."

Jake's mother came to the phone, and I explained who I am, and we spoke briefly. She said, "I know you, Jake told me about you, and let me thank you for being so kind to my son." I smile, not from my own joy of recognition, but because hopefully my presence and God's grace had intervened to save someone else's child.

See, I did nothing. God protected that child as he protects me and you. If we have the opportunity to help someone whose path we cross, maybe it was divine intervention. I believe that. I didn't impact anyone in these stories; they impacted me. How did God send me Jake around the same time Taylor laid down for his final sleep? Why did he put these boys in my path? I smile today, and I know it is to tell this story to others, to help show each of us that divine intervention starts with us.

A few years after this story, I bought my first motorcycle. The guy I bought it from had helmets for sale, and I thought of buying one of the less expensive ones. He said, "You had better think. If you want to save that pretty face of yours, you need this one with a shield." I smiled and picked out one that cost a bit more but included a face shield. I laughed out loud at those words and their impact because after this man said that to me, my memory went right back to that night with Jake. He said, "What's so funny?"

I told him, "It's a long story, but you are right. I do like my face, and I shall protect it."

God gave me peace that day with that bike, and I learned a creed with bikers that only bikers understand, same as only true Christians understand. We all bond to those who feel like we do, love like we do, and thank God like we all need to do.

Chapter 3:

Crumbs of Life

Often I reflect and use the phrase "crumbs of life." I came to use phrase while dating a man that would barely fit me into his schedule. I was only getting the crumbs of his time, as I liked to phrase it. I knew I deserved more, but for some reason I settled for it during an adversity in life that I was barely surmounting. Yet as always, God showed me his humor and spoke to me, explaining that sometimes we only get crumbs. For some, sadly, those crumbs are all they have available during their hardships.

I often reflect upon a homeless lady that I often saw in California. She lived under a bridge with a shopping cart full of crumbs others had given her or that she had accumulated while searching for necessities. Several times I would pull over into a parking lot and look at her life through my eyes. I thought, "How does one get this way at this stage in life? Does she have children that have no idea where she is, or how is she surviving, or does anyone from childhood like a sister or brother even care?"

As I looked at her face, which to me is like a map of life's journey, I could see that she was older. Her skin showed hard-pressed lines that stuck together; similar to pinching skin together, and it is sticking together from the dryness of the climate here.

Often when I see this on someone, I think they are heavy smokers, heavy drinkers, or damaged from tanning under the rays of sun, which we once thought was beautiful. Unfortunately, that temporary beauty of youth is no longer there. The consequence of trying to be beautiful for summer's wardrobe has branded most with this texture of skin.

As I watch her existence, I am amazed at her survival skills. I decide that she is a survivor most will never understand, and has been through more than most will experience. Most will ignore her and think she deserves it, or that she is beneath us. Some will say if we give her our crumbs, then we have done our part, and will drive away thinking that they have done something great.

I decided right then, that the next day I would bring her gifts. I left my parking lot with that in mind. I noticed then that, not only does she have herself, but she also has a dog and most of us would think, I wonder how she can feed a dog with barely enough for herself. I drove away thinking how some days she must be so blessed to be loved.

Sadly, when I took my gifts to the homeless lady, she was gone. After seeing her so many times daily I thought I would have the time to talk to her. It was not to be

So today, I open my back door, and there is my neighbor's dog. This golden retriever weighs more than I, yet he settles for any crumbs of food, love, or warmth that I can give. I lay his towel down and he comes in. It doesn't matter how he smells, what I do or say, or what I feed him; all he wants is his treat and play time with me. I gave him crumbs of his snack, when he obeyed my command not to push me over. My home is a tin box with barely enough room for me. As I watch him sleep on his side, the memory of the homeless lady comes to mind. I know her struggles even though I am not homeless. I know her love for this precious gift with a heartbeat that knows nothing but love. Beyond anything, I understand the crumbs that are welcomed in my life. Jesus asked in Matthew 6:26, "Is you're worth not more than a bird?" A bird is thankful for crumbs; survival depends on crumbs, and it never worries about anything. Jesus also asks, "If a broken sparrow falls to the ground and the other is in his palm, is one better than the other?"

I can answer that with my own life and what Jesus would say. He would say, "You of great strength, you of great faith, help the broken one to get back up and fly." We owe Jesus the privilege of helping those who are broken, and when we are broken, he gently places us in the palm of his hand.

Love all, be kind, because at some point in life, crumbs are what we too shall have. Whether it's the last hours of someone we love's time; whether it be the loss of everything we have feared in life to come full circle and we are broken; or whether it be in the character we display walking in love as Christ did. Our crumbs will be all we ask for, and they will be plenty.

I now wonder if the homeless lady was but a disciple of God, and I didn't even give her my crumbs. I ask forgiveness, and I write this story so you, too, may see.

Chapter 4:

Friday Night Lights

Don't ask me why I love Fridays. I have since childhood; however, many sad things have happened to me on Fridays. One Friday I was working at the ER, and a call came in saying that we were to receive a patient from an auto accident. Within minutes this patient was in the trauma room. Because it was a small ER, these traumas seldom stopped there and were instead flown to a trauma facility. This day there were two people involved in the accident. One person was flown out, and the other one was sent to us. She was sent to us because she was beyond any hope of survival.

We received her with an artificial airway in place, called a ventilator tube, because when the paramedics arrived she was not breathing. She most likely died upon impact. There was nothing we could do to save her. The ER was buzzing with the events of the day that began this end to a life.

There was so much anger from those who brought her inside. Anger about the destruction she chose to cause under these bright Friday night lights that come with being in a small town. One complaint is from the paramedic who brought her in. I take him to the side and ask him, "Where is the compassion here?"

His voice is raised and full of anger that I am sure I will understand at another time. This lady, Joni, whose body I saw in the distance woke up earlier that day and went with her boyfriend to another state about fifty miles from home. They ate at a local chain, which I still go to at times. Each time I stop there, before entering its doors, I remember that this was where she ate her last meal. I often wonder if I am in the same seat that she had chosen on her last day on earth.

The paramedic explains that she, and this boyfriend decided to rob a bank after that meal. After leaving the bank, there was a car chase involving every patrol car in the area. As they drove onto the interstate, I can only imagine what happened.

During the chase, road blocks were set in place to keep them from crossing state lines as they headed east toward their home. Upon seeing this, she made a decision to cross the median going at a high rate of speed. As they crossed over, because their SUV's weight and the speed at which they were driving, the SUV's front bumper hit the indention in the median. The car stopped and flipped. It also did something like a nose dive, hitting the hard concrete. During the crash, she and her boyfriend ejected instantly through the back of the SUV, where I am sure life ended for Joni.

I speak to the young medic and say, "Why are you so angry?"

He said, "Do you know how many cops risked their lives in this pursuit? What if it was your son and he was in the midst of this?" I never understood that, but looking back now I wonder if his dad may have been in law enforcement; if he had a brother or a friend who was injured or killed in a pursuit like this. I have learned that when anger surfaces, it is usually from past pains in life. Without knowing his battles in life, I had no right to judge him, or this lady lying lifeless on the table.

After everyone left the ER and the drama and trauma moved out of the ER, I walked into the trauma room. Now understand, seeing death is not something I am good at as a nurse. Why God placed me in this position in life I only understand now. It is maybe so that I can understand how thankful and blessed I am to write this story.

As I walked into the trauma room, I had a saltine cracker that I was eating. I taste the salt and feel its texture absorb the saliva inside my mouth. I gently turned back the sheet and looked at Joni. I realized that I am in the healing phase of understanding death, destruction, and despair. I could only see Joni's head, so I pulled back the sheet to look at the region where her heart once had beat. I noticed a name along with a date tattooed on her skin. Based on the date, this child is small. She carried this child's heartbeat nine months. Now I am looking upon the region where her heart stopped and see the name of this child. I no longer taste the salt of the saltine cracker, instead I taste the salt from the tears that are rolling down my cheeks and landing on my lips.

My heart was heavy because I thought of what this child would be told that day, and how Fridays may never be her favorite day of the week again. I cried silently for her life and for the family Joni left behind with such a bad choice that day. I asked God to help this family through this difficult time, and I thanked him for the safety he provided those in the pursuit of life's elements.

This story reminds me not to judge others; to understand people's anger; and to tell everyone I speak to or cross paths with, that I love them; whether it be with words, actions, or in the form of a smile. I am thankful to the God I serve and the God that has protected me so many times.

Joni's boyfriend was air lifted to a trauma unit and died a few days later. As I write this story, the Holy Spirit embraces me and says that Joni is ok. Being a mom myself, and having made many bad choices in my life, I believe at the end, she asked God to forgive her, as we all would do in a life or death situation. Had she lived, she would have been in prison most of her child's life. I believe with every ounce of faith that I have that she was taken to keep her child from having to suffer for her wrongs in life. Sadly, all of us still endure wrongs done to us by others. It is the circle of life, and we each get a choice to make a difference or to be the difference.

What shall you do with your Fridays? I shall smile; I shall thank God for the day; I will feel grace from his presence; and I will write each story that I can to show each of us that we all matter to someone. Some we know, and some we briefly pass by. I can say I have been in the midst of death all my life, and a few times I have held the hands of those that passed.

Chapter 5:

Close to Home

I wasn't a part of this story so much as a nurse, but more so as a parent. I experienced the bonding of parents during a tragedy on graduation night. Being both an ER nurse and a mom, I have seen tragedies on many graduation nights and prom nights and how they can change the course of many lives. My son was graduating from high school, and me being a mom, who always tried to capture life in a photo, wanted pictures.

Of course William was like, "Mom, enough," because he is ready to go out for the party.

I remember my reply verbatim. I said, "William, look around this room at this moment. There is a good chance someone's life will change tonight. They may not be here tomorrow, or there could be an event that changes every one of your friend's lives. So soak it in; let me get my pictures."

One of the last pictures I was about to take was of William, his friend Henley, and his best friend since childhood Derrick. I shot that frame and couldn't wait to develop my pictures the next day. William rushed to go to the party at a nearby house where many would end up that night. I silently prayed for my son and his friends' safety, knowing that they had the capacity to make poor choices. Looking back, maybe I shouldn't have been so lenient, but like most parents I allowed this. I was thinking we couldn't do anything; they were just being kids. It was the wrong choice.

I called William a few minutes after eleven o'clock to see how he was and told him that I was going to bed. He had no idea that sleep would not happen for me that night because of my experiences in ER. Actually, more staff is now placed in ER and on ambulances in certain places on nights like these because of the influx of kids being rolled in by EMR.

I laid down, but only managed a few hours of sleep that night. I took extra precautions and had my cell phone and the landline phone right beside my bed. I often awoke just to check the phone. I could have overdosed on bedtime meds and still been awake that night. That is only a metaphor, but with the intensity of my alertness, nothing could have shut down my worry.

Around seven in the morning, my cell phone rang. It was William and his voice was wracked with fear. He said, "Mom you have to get to the hospital. Call anyone you know; we think Jason is dead." He continues to explain the previous night's events. He had awoken up cold and unable to sleep. Many were lying around on the floor because there weren't enough beds. He had called his uncle to come and get him around two in the morning.

A few minutes after six in the morning, Derrick and two other boys woke up and headed to town to get something to eat. On their way, Derrick crashes the car. Jason, who was a friend from out of town, was thrown from the vehicle. Jason was a hemophiliac which is a disorder where people's blood does not clot properly. If they get cut or have trauma, they have a greater incidence of death than most people do.

My son was so frightened, and since I was a nurse, I knew many people in the area. He knew that I could find out what had happened. William's dad and I headed to the ER. As I walked through these doors for the first time as a visitor, I noticed many parents were in the side room, and I headed that way.

I spoke to one of the doctors who worked there, but he, like I, was also on the other side today. I looked at him and said, "Phillip, what's going on?"

He replied, "All we know is that Derrick is in critical shape; the other boy in the car has minor injuries; and Jason hasn't been brought in yet." Phillip's eyes and my eyes locked. We knew what not being transported to the ER meant. There are only two reasons someone isn't brought in: either he refused, or he was dead. We both knew which it was, based on Jason's medical condition. Since Jason was from out of town, no one knew his parents. We all knew that we would know them the moment they arrived.

I looked around the room and noticed my good friend, Henley's mom, and I reached for her. I also looked for the familiar face of my son, but I did not find him. I attempted to call him and when there was no answer, I became frightened. I noticed Henley approaching me, and I asked him where William was. He told me that he thinks William may also have been in the car. My heart dropped. I couldn't breathe, and I start to tear up.

Then I said, "No I talked to him, and he called his uncle to come and get him this morning." But my first reaction was to think how this could have been my son. It put me in the shoes of the other parents in that room, full of vulnerability, compassion, sadness, and uncertainty.

As my lungs start to inhale again, I smelled the familiar scent of the cologne my son wears. I turned and hugged him. He asked if we knew anything and I told him, "Jason still hasn't been brought in." Both William and Henley know what that means, and I said, "I don't think it's good."

The little crowd that had gathered there became a big crowd. Derrick's family was with him as they continued the life support that had been started on him at the scene. I was sure that they were praying as they had never prayed before; consumed with worry for their own son, and the others in the wreck. Every parent in the room was supported by the friendships of our children, our shared concern for Jason, and our anticipation of his parent's arrival. None of us knew what they would look like when they did appear. Little did I know, I would never see his parents.

Phillip left the room and came back a few minutes later, explaining that Derrick was about to be sent to the ICU. He also confirmed that Jason had died the moment he was ejected from the car. A cross would later be placed where he had landed. Each of us as parents bowed our heads. We prayed for this child; this family; and the events of the last twenty-four hours that would forever alter their lives.

I don't think any of us wanted to see Jason's parents. In a moment like this, there are no words; there is no support, no wisdom, no understanding, and nothing that we could offer. It is the most helpless feeling to be present for the moments that change lives.

After praying, some started gathering their things. The youth decided to hang around for Derrick, and I just wanted get out. I did not want to be in the particles of life that had ended for such a young man. Henley and William were broken; all Derrick's friends were wounded to the cores of their souls; and all of us parents were thanking God that it wasn't our child. We were frightened at the news that Jason's parents would be told.

As we gathered our mental bearings of thoughts and worries, we heard a scream that you have only heard in movies. Each of us froze. Maybe it is a sound that you thought you, yourself, would make if you had lost a child; as if you felt the pain, as if every chamber of your heart was being ripped from its cavity, one fiber at a time. Time froze for everyone in this side room of ER.

We couldn't see what the owner of the voice looked like, but from its tone of pain we each knew that it was Jason's mother. I do not think the movies can begin to capture the sound of such pain. I had heard it many times, but today, it was different. Today, it could have been my son. It could have been my best friend's son. I do not think one mother hasn't at one time in her life feared that they, too, may experience something this terrible. When you love someone this much, it is normal to have such fears and such thoughts.

I can say I dislike that sound, and I always stop and seek out those with this scream. I think that if I am lucky, maybe I will not hear it again. I did, however, many times after this day. But that day will always stay captured inside my collage of life. No one in that room will ever forget that sound, or that loss. That day the course of life changed for each of us, especially for Jason's family, and for Derrick, who lost much of his mental capacity that day. Maybe God allowed that so he wouldn't carry the burden of being the driver of the vehicle that day. Maybe he couldn't have coped, except within the limits that he was left with at this time; I don't know. Derrick was in the hospital many months and was later transferred to a Neurological hospital to get him back up to functional capacity. His friends often made trips to see him. Derrick's short-term memory was forever altered that day. Years later, Derrick would show up at our door at five in the morning and stay for hours. The way he had remembered it, William's dad was an early riser.

Sadly for all of us there that day, that blood curdling scream, and the loss of a child will forever be in our minds. These things help us to find empathy, understand vulnerability, remain humble, and forever mold our children into the beginning of becoming an adult.

I cherish that last picture still today of Henley, Derrick, and William. Little did I know to say those words to William, or to freeze this frame of the last day that any one of these three boys was while still in high school.

Then again, maybe God just told me. I know that these moments, frozen within the frames of life, often have a meaning that God wants to show us later. Nine years later, as I write this story, I think He knew.

Chapter 6:

Last Flight of Hope

After spending many years traveling on and off planes, when I returned home from one of my trips, like always I was exhausted. It would usually take me several days to get over these flights, and the more than eighty-hour weeks I worked so I could be at be home with my son. The day after arriving home from one of my trips, I received a call from a friend who owned a travel nurse company. He asked if I would be willing to fly on a corporate plane with a twenty-seven year old to MD Anderson.

He told me there was no pay involved, but he would cover the expenses incurred in order to help this friend out. I was tired and wanted to stay home, but then he informed me of the story. He said, "I have asked over one hundred nurses to fly with this family to MD Anderson, and because there is no pay, no one will go." The words hit me with how sad it was that people wouldn't give their time with no pay. It was on this trip that I learned time has no price. Some moments we give to others, and they become a story to be told, and the pay is a lifetime of learning about the handprints on our hearts.

Jason was twenty-seven years old. He had been diagnosed with glioblastoma, an aggressive kind of brain tumor. At the time, I didn't know much about anything to do with cancer or the wrath of its aggression. Also, I did

Last Flight of Hope

not know that this would be Jason's last flight, and my first one inside a corporate plane.

Jason's dad had worked as a high-ranking employee at a corporation. They had loaned their plane and its crew of two pilots as well. I showed up at the appointed place the next day, without a clue of what I would do if anything happened. I was actually just supposed to be present to help the family emotionally. I don't know that I helped this family, but I can say by the grace of God and this trip, I was helped.

As I stepped into the private terminal, the two pilots kindly greeted me. One seemed nicer than the other, and looking back now, I remember that one of them had two children and the other had none.

A car pulled in as I was being greeted and out stepped Jason's parents. In the back seat of the car was this young man who was weak and cold. He was wrapped in a baby blue blanket. His dad opened the door and Jason, being the grace of a young man, smiles as much as he is able to at this stage in cancer's wrath.

His dad and the one of the two pilots helped him out of the car. Slowly, he walked up the narrow set of steps to board this flight. He had to be helped, but he mustered up every ounce of energy that he could to make it and then collapsed into the seat closest to the door. He could not have walked another step. From the appearance of Jason, I can tell he is as exhausted, as if he had walked hundreds of miles in extreme conditions. Actually the conditions that he was fighting at that time were extreme, but I did not know this then. After we took off, I was informed of the story. Jason had been diagnosed with this cancer for less than a year. It took its vengeance with the speed of fire as wind fuels its path.

I spoke to Jason, but I could see that he was weak and tired, and that he just wanted to sleep. I looked over toward his dad. Knowing men as I do today, his heart was heavy; his spirit was broken; and his love was captured in the worry lines that showed on his face. It was a look that I had later in life, too. Jason's mother was directly across from me, and I looked to her. I knew the love between a mother and son. My son was only thirteen at the time, and all my life had been dedicated to spending time with him. I can remember stopping at red lights and bursting into tears from loving him so much. I just asked God to let me live long enough to see him grown, and as I write this story today, he is twenty-seven years old. You think God didn't have meaning and purpose for my life and this family?

If anyone reading this has ever flown in a corporate plane, you will understand they are small and contained to the point that I thought I could feel the chill of Jason's breath; the perfume of his mom's softness; and the musky smell of a his dad who was stressed to the breaking point about not being able to fix his child.

Looking back, little did I know that my son's father would have this same fear about his son, and that I would know what Jason's mother was feeling. Thinking about it still gives me chills, and from being in the presence of God, knowing how we all get our time in life to relive moments that we all at some point shall go through in life.

I looked at Jason and saw that he was sleeping; his dad was absorbed in his thoughts and worry while looking out at the clouds, and his mom begins to tell me of Jason.

Jason had been to college; he had a girlfriend he planned to marry; and life was going good for him. Then symptoms of this disease began to surface, and once he was diagnosed, life as he and his parents had planned it, ceased.

They were flying to MD Anderson as a last hope. The prognosis wasn't good, and they would be informed if there was any hope for Jason. Without hope, all life stops for brief moments or a lifetime. Hope is our faith; it is our humbleness; and it is when we rely on God and prayer as we never have before. Without hope, our light becomes darkness, and the ability to shine stagnates from mourning the loss of hope.

His mom told me that he would most likely die, but she was not ready to give up, so they were making this last fight of hope. She told me stories of Jason as a child, as a teenager, and now as a young man. I listened not just to let her vent but to understand the meaning of this child's life no knowing that one day it, too, would parallel my last fight of hope in years to come.

I looked at Jason and noticed his baby blue blanket had fallen on the floor as he had fallen asleep. I reached to pick it up, and I inhaled its soft scent. I understand that most have never smelled softness, but I can always smell its fragrance. I place the blanket over Jason and continue to inhale the scents of a mom's pain; a father's worry, and my heart wanted to hold my own son. I silently thank God for giving me a son.

As we arrived in Texas, we were greeted as soon as the door opened. Jason was taken to a car waiting nearby, and the pilots and I were ushered to our hotel. Let me say this about being in a private plane—you are treated with luxury upon arrival with a fast departure, and everything that money can buy. However, I wouldn't have traded my lifestyle for what this family was enduring. Their greatest gifts were their children. Jason's father worked hard, and his company rewarded his pain with comfort and speed on his last flight.

The two pilots and I arrived at the hotel. We went to dinner and made plans to fly home the next day. We spoke of the day's events, and we asked each other many questions. We each went to our rooms and planned to meet for breakfast the next morning to wait for the time of departure.

Upon entering my room, I couldn't wait to call home. I wanted to hold my son so badly that I started crying, and being this strong independent woman, I didn't want my husband to know I hurt. I made the call and told my husband a small amount of the day's events. He didn't comment, and looking back, I understand that he just didn't understand my depth or my flight in life.

I asked to speak to our son, and he came to the phone. I asked about his day, and he responded. Since he was almost fourteen, he was at that independent phase, not wanting to show emotion or seem to care. As we said goodbye, we told each other, "I love you." I learned long ago to never leave home without telling my son I loved him. This just humbled me to remind others.

The next morning was brisk and cool, especially for the state of Texas. We were informed that we would have to stay another night. We all ventured out to the Holocaust Museum there, to see the destruction Hitler caused to so many. I think we all shed tears that day. I would have to say that Hitler was a walking form of cancer as his cancer spread with each person's life he took during at war. It was a solemn day, and after we finished, we again had dinner and went to our rooms. I called home again, never allowing my family to see my pain. I ended my day with voice of my son—priceless.

The next morning we gathered our things and stayed at the hotel until we were notified that Jason and his family were ready. We went to the airport, and again, let me say that the treatment of those with money compared to those without, is vast. I am thankful for my humbleness, and I am thankful for those of wealth who donate luxury, so it has two good sides.

As I boarded, all were in place. Jason had changed so much in two days. He couldn't speak or walk, just his body was present. He was wrapped in a thicker blanket from the hospital, and his mom held his light blue blanket from our first trip, inhaling the scent of her child. His dad looked as if he had aged five years in two days, and I was a shadow among the clouds, silently thanking God for my son.

Jason's mom said he didn't have long to live. I just took her hand and watched the last flight of hope disappear from their lives. When we arrived back home and reached the terminal, Jason's body was weak, and he was unable to even open his eyes. He was carried off that plane and placed in the back seat of the car he arrived in, only this time he was in his mother's arms.

I thanked the pilots, took their emails, and emailed with them for a few years, but we lost contact through the years.

I arrived home, and the first thing I did was hug my son and inhale hope, love, and the smell of my child.

Two days after arriving home, Jason's dad called to say he had died. I remember going to the funeral home and having to wait in line to see the family. I was greeted with a hug of sorrow, thankfulness, and gratitude that one hundred other nurses turned down. Not being paid for this journey was the best thing to ever happen to me. My reward is this story and the humbleness Jason's life taught me. Looking back, being a part of this flight, no paycheck I could receive is even close to the value of life I learned those days. I was so blessed to absorb, to contribute, and to acknowledge Jason's last flight on earth.

Chapter 7:

Lifetime Love

Today I saw an elderly man sitting at his wife's bedside. His head was hung as low as physically possible. His hands were clasped and crossed, as men do when they are thinking. He was broken, lonely, and sad beyond what words could express. I saw this brokenness as I passed his room and went to my destination, but again I knew I had to know this story as well. Why did I notice this?

At the time, the ER is filled with non-life-threatening situations. The doctors were writing orders, and others were just waiting to be seen. Not one person was taking the time to see the uncertainty in this man, so I walked into the room, and I began to talk to him. Even the timbre of his voice was broken and tears sat in his eyes. I asked him what happened, and he told me the most beautiful story.

He said, "Today is our fifty-fifth wedding anniversary, and my wife had cooked dinner. As we sat down to eat, she looked at me and fell to the floor, and I called 911. I don't know anything except the doctors say it is bad."

I asked his permission to go and ask, since she was not my patient. He said, "Yes."

He grabbed my hand, and said, "Thank you." I went to the doctor, and he explained that the lady had had a stroke.

A stroke is a hemorrhagic bleed and hers was in the worst spot on the brain to have such. It is as if a water facet is turned on and fills the head with blood. With the skull being so hard, it has no time to be reabsorbed and no room to expand. Brain death is imminent because it cuts off the blood supply.

The woman was already on a ventilator, and her brain was most certainly dead. I knew this and I went back to speak with this man. I told him the truth in the simple terms I described above. I asked him what she was like; how many kids they had; and what he loved the most about her. He replied with great pride and told me of their life together and their three children and five grandchildren. What struck me the most were the tears that fell from his eyes as he said, "I have never spent a day without her, how will I now?" I could not answer this question or even begin to understand being loved by a man this much. Knowing love like this existed gave me faith, whether it be for fifty-five years or for five. I do know that with God's love I am complete, with friends and faith I am loved, and most importantly, I daily, as we all do, have the opportunity to see, feel, touch, and become a part of this world.

With God we are given gifts to use. As I left this man with tears in my eyes, he thanked me multiple times. I looked at him and said, "No, thank you for your time." This man thought I was helping him, but the fact is, we were helping each other. He showed me hope, faith, and that love is there no matter the years I have left.

For people that take one day for granted know it too shall change. I remember a greeting card I bought my first time in England that stated, "Live each day as if it were your last, because one day it will be true."

How great could our lives be if people only applied this to our busy lives? Can we not take fifteen minutes to give to God, to give to ourselves, and to give to others? If not, they too, shall pass, and we will never get that back.

My prayer for you today is to stop, look, and listen. Be good to yourself. Tell someone that you love them and listen to a story, and most of all, give Jesus his time, for he gave his life for you. Don't you think we owe him more than fifteen minutes?

Chapter 8:

Never Give Up

It wasn't long after working a few years as a nurse that I started doing travel nursing with my friend Margaret. She and I rode back and forth to nursing school every day. She instantly became one of my best friends. She convinced me to travel, so off we went to California. I had never been anywhere except on vacation to Florida or the Caribbean. Going to California, made me feel as if I was going to the movies. We both got accepted at the same hospital and lived out of a Holiday Inn for four weeks. By this time, I had advanced from surgical floor to ICU and floated to step-down unit. So, on different days, I worked in different areas.

It was in ICU that I meet this amazing man, Jimmy. He had a wife and a daughter who was the same age as my son. He was on life support and dying from alcoholism. At that time, I did not understand the impact this would have on me eighteen years later. Jimmy had basically drunk himself into a coma. His liver had stopped working, and the doctors were trying to explain to his wife and his parents that, even if he lived, it would not be good. This family was adamant that they were not going to give up on Jimmy. He was only thirty-seven years old: a father, a husband and a son. There was no way they were going to take him off the ventilator.

I became close to the family that day and was on their side in this issue because I was in this age group as well. As I left ICU that night after work, the family stopped and hugged me, telling me how thankful they were. Of course I was thinking, "I am a good nurse and did a good job that day."

I was off work for the next two days, and when I returned, I floated to the step-down unit, which is a unit where you are not stable enough to go to the floor but stable enough to be on this unit. Your nurse to patient ratio is approximately three-to-one versus six-to-one, so you get more of the nurse's time. Well, what were the chances that I would get the patient I did? Yes, it was Jimmy! He had progressed enough so that he was off the ventilator, but he was still in really bad health. He was lethargic; his abdomen was huge; and the color of his skin was the color best described as a dark tan with a tint of yellow—jaundice. You could tell because his eyes were yellow and his skin stank of a sweating odor that comes with cirrhosis.

The family was proud they did not give up on him, and I was enlightened as well. As the day progressed, Jimmy started getting worse. I called the doctors numerous times, and I explained he had to go back into ICU and on a ventilator because he was a full code. This means that you have to fight to the last breath to save a person. I had two other patients, but most of my day was spent battling to keep on top of Jimmy's condition.

Around four in the afternoon, they took him to ICU and started the process again. Over the course of a few weeks, this battle continued. Each day that I worked, the family asked for me to be the nurse, and there was a bond there only we understood. One of the doctors pulled me aside one day and said, "I need you to tell this family he is not going to make it. We cannot fix everyone, but for some reason they believe in you." He continued, "You know this outcome. Please help us out."

Sadly, I did know the outcome or thought that I knew. I went and spoke with the patient, his wife and his mom. I explained what the doctor had said to me, and I asked if we could make him a no code. This meant that if he didn't turn around, there was nothing left to do. It is in this moment that I realized I was a stranger to this bond of faith, love, loyalty, and determination I was not a part of in this family circle. In other words, "No."

To be honest, I thought my assessment and that of the doctors was correct; however, it was not my call. I had only two days left to work on my contract, so the family took my email address. They bought me this adorable angel, which I treasure beyond any gift ever given to me. My last day at work I handed them my cell number and asked them to keep in touch.

About four months later, I got a card in the mail. It was a picture of Jimmy at home, using a walker and being placed on the transplant list for a liver. He was living life as best he could. A few months later, I got an email telling me that he was off the transplant list and now was back at work. I remember that day as if it were today. I realized how quickly we give up on others based on someone else's opinion. These people had faith; they had love; and they had a bond unbroken in this world of man that we live in today. My heart still skips a beat, not believing he would survive. Isn't this how God is? When everyone else gives up, He doesn't. We should never live a day in this life without faith; and if we have it we should walk in it, stand up for it, and most of all, believe in it. Hebrews 11:1 teaches us this. This was a life lesson for me, and it should be one for all who are reading this now. Do not give up. Have faith. And do not ever fail to listen to that gut instinct, which is the Holy Spirit saying, "I've got this one for you."

My prayer for you today is to believe in yourself; believe in God; and most of all, believe in faith.

Chapter 9:

No Answer to Some Whys

One night I was working the intensive care unit. As with all critical care patients being flown in to the hospital, there was a doctor there to receive the patient. Based on the events leading up to the tragedy, the paramedics relayed what they had found when they arrived and the patient's status. From there, the nurse sets up the ICU room with the equipment needed. We got a call involving a young lady around the age of twenty-three. Lily had attempted suicide. The way she tried to embrace death still lingers in the heart of my soul, showing how much despair truly is among us.

Lily and her boyfriend, Jon, had begun a fight earlier in the afternoon. She did not want him to go to work. She did not want to be left alone. Remembering myself at this age and the limited coping skills and experiences that I had, I tried to understand this pain. Eventually, the fight lead to him leaving to go to work. As he walked out the door, she locked all the doors and ran to her bedroom. Jon said he turned back to go check on her, but found his key to the home was not on his key ring. She had removed them because she had planned out the scenario in case he left.

He went to the bedroom window, and what he saw I am sure was the ending of a life no young man should ever see. It was also the beginning of guilt beyond any shame one this age should carry into their future. He noticed Lily hanging from the closet rod. The shadows of her body still in motion from the impact of pain's weight only few shall see in this lifetime.

Jon broke in through the window, laid her on the floor, and called 911. When the call came into ICU, each person with empathy inside the walls of the ICU stopped and wondered how, why, and will she make it. None of them understand this method of attempt. Some have anger fueled by the senselessness of such an attempt, and then others begin to identify its origin in pain. It's just the only way some learn to cope, and others just shut down because God protects them from seeing the forms of death we see so often. Well, with me, I now look back and reflect that God stamped this story on my collage of life as a memory to share.

As Lily arrived in the ICU, I thought that I was ready to see this woman. Nothing in a movie, life, or my memory was prepared for what I saw. Lily was a petite woman, and she looked as if she were blessed with external beauty; a smile that would light up anyone's day; and possibly a woman any man would gravitate to. At least, that is my perception based on her superficial appearance.

That night she lay before me, and what I saw as a nurse was not the same as what I described. She was broken, unconscious, and on a ventilator. The temperature of her body was elevated to an extreme that would eventually lead to seizures, possibly brain death, and the end of her physical life on earth. Her skull expanded to twice the size it should be; her eyes bulged to the point that they had to be taped shut to stop them from protruding from their sockets; her neck was swollen and bruised from the indentation marks left by the rope. It has its own shadows left from the swaying motion inside that closet from the previous hours of despair. Lily makes it through the night, yet as I left the next morning, I left with humbleness and sorrow. I think sadly about what Jon, her parents, and her family and friends must face today when they visit. They will pray like they have never prayed before; they will hope; and they will carry the guilt and shame of not seeing this coming. I know this because in my life I carry a similar burden from the suicide of someone I knew.

It is from those traits that I write this to the family, friends and all involved with suicide and the uncertainty of the whys in life. I first wrote this in the form of a card to send someone who lost a loved one to suicide. Today, I use it to help you to understand you have to forgive yourself and them.

We wonder why so often in life, why does someone take their own life and to leave for generations the fear and the wondering of why? There is no answer. Loved ones, family, and friends that do this have no answers as to why. They are mentally, emotionally, and spiritually dying. They are at the end of their ropes in life, and they feel that there is only one choice which was to give up on life.

We don't need to know why as much as we need to remember the impact they had on our lives. I am sorry for your loss. There is no answer you can find except forgiveness within. Let go of any whys today. Remember their hearts, remember their smiles and the greatness they brought to your life, and love them, but first forgive them.

You didn't contribute to his/her death, and it is not your burden to carry. God is peace, and with suicide that was their only way to find peace from pain. Never would they want you to carry their burden. It is a choice they made from the depth of their pain; the emotional anguish they didn't want others to see; and it may not be the right thing to do, but sometimes in life, we give up on hope. We give up on ourselves and then we sink into a darkness for just a moment that changes the course of life for everyone left behind.

So today, I ask that you not to judge them or yourself; let go of the why. Don't blame yourself. Find peace that God is in your life, and he will bring you peace and the answers that you need to know about the whys. He showed me after thirty-three years. You get to decide how many years it shall take you. If you give it to God sooner, it may not take that many years of your life.

I don't know the outcome of Lily or her family. I know from my medical knowledge that she died that night at the end of her rope. God protected me, so I could walk away from not knowing why. That day, Lily's story started part of my journey to the destiny God wants me to have. That destiny is peace in knowing that I truly never have to carry the guilt, shame, or responsibility for others' choices, only my own. Once I find forgiveness, I am blessed with peace, empathy, and the understanding of what is left for me to carry forward to help others to know that there are some whys we don't need the answer to in this life.

Chapter 10:

Power of Words

When I began nursing school, my full intent was to be a Pharmaceutical Sales Representative and not actually an RN. I loved sales and thought this was my ticket in to this field, yet God as always, has a sense of humor. If you aren't the size of a model, it is hard to break in to this field, so I became a nurse.

I began college, and prior to being accepted, I met Maggie. Maggie was in one of the same classes as me, and we became instant friends. We were both accepted to nursing school at the same time. Maggie was overweight, as was I a bit, and was the single mother of two girls. She and I studied together; she rode to school with me each day. Throughout all this time, I understood that a friendship like this was to be shared and cherished. We helped each other through many trials in life, and for that I am blessed.

During nursing school, I gained sixty pounds and Maggie that much or more, simply from stress eating and other unhealthy eating habits. Food was our external force that brought senses alive as we were enduring some of the toughest years of our lives. It happens, and you just go on with life and endure the consequences of the judgmental labels of society. Aside from the devaluing we felt of ourselves, we had to endure glances of disgust, misunderstanding, stereotypes from others, and the self-loathing that I believe most women encounter at some time in their life.

Maggie was much larger than me, but her heart was kind and larger than any scale could weigh. She often was misunderstood and rejected. She had a bad marriage and had made some of the bad choices that we all make in life. It made her strong with the bitterness of actually just not caring unless you touched the right emotion. A touchy subject for her was her weight and how she devalued herself.

Maggie and I made it through nursing school and kind of took a break from each other. Her reason was that I always went for the underdog and seemed to not take her side. During this time, losing this friendship was like a death sentence to me. I survived, and a few years later, she called and asked me to start doing travel nursing with her. I agreed, and off we went to many states and places and events few would ever see. Our friendship took a new turn, and we grew an even greater appreciation of each other.

On one occasion we flew out of a small airport into a larger city to catch a direct flight to our destination. Little did I know, this day would have a profound, devastating result for Maggie. Looking back as I write this today, I now understand the power of words even more. I must warn everyone reading this that your words have the potential to bring change and destruction forever. So always be careful when you speak words, especially if they are unkind.

This plane we boarded was small, and the weight limits are always an issue with small planes. The flight crew announced the flight was over-weight for takeoff. They stated that they were shifting luggage and people around. Because Maggie was at the front of the plane, she was asked to move to the right side of the plane. She did as she was instructed. The captain offered a voucher for one person to take; however, no one wanted to spend the day at the airport for any amount of money. Eventually, the captain said that all was shifted, and we would be taking off.

The doors were closed; the plane engine started; and the flight was about to take off just slightly off schedule.

As the plane was about to start its normal take off procedure; following the federal regulations; the flight attendant, who was barely a size four, maybe around thirty, and extremely cute, noticed that Maggie didn't have her seatbelt on. Maggie whispered to her that it would not fit around her. This cute, small-framed lady echoed her words with a tone of contempt. She turned to the pilot and said, "We have to have to seatbelt extension for this woman. The plane's doesn't fit her. She is too big for the seat."

I know she was doing her job, but the way she handled it still gives me goose bumps. Maggie was humiliated. They had to call the technicians to find a seatbelt extender, which took around fifteen minutes and that meant the door had to be reopened, and the seatbelt manually brought to the plane. From the reactions of some on the plane, you could tell they were so irritated and the whispers began. Tears fell from my eyes and created a small stream of salty water as I hurt for my friend. I understood her pain, humiliation, and most of all her fear of attention because of the weight.

After all this was completed, the plane took off. The flight attendant came to me to ask if I wanted a soft drink, and I just turned my head to keep from seeing the ugliness. It was in that moment that I understood beauty from the surface has no beauty without love beneath. I cringed to even see a beautiful woman that speaks only based on her external physical appearance, compared to what she is internally. Love always makes us beautiful. If we are blessed with God's internal beauty, we feel grace throughout life.

As we landed in the larger city and deplaned, I caught up with my friend. I found her in the bathroom crying and humiliated from the harsh words of someone having a bad day, or just being cruel. Granted, the flight attendant was doing her job, but she did it without any grace or love. This lady placed a scar in the lining of Maggie's heart that impacted her to the day she died.

Maggie brought up that situation from time to time in the years to come, and the bitterness in her words became even stronger as years passed us by.

Many years later, she lost weight, and she went to get her bachelors of Science degree, and she was working on her master's degree the year she died. I remember the day so vividly that I am just now to the point of letting her go. My son was sick; I had just filed for a divorce; and Maggie's life was going in a downward spiral of tiredness based on our talks. The last five months of her life, we didn't talk because I was in such despair in my own life, and each time we called each other, life seemed to get in the way.

My sister and I were packing up belongings in my home to be moved, and we were sitting outside. It was around 9:30 pm, and a helicopter flew over my patio. I saw the lights and knew it was a medical helicopter. I looked to God and said, "Lord, please be with this family as they are going through this crisis." I had no idea why I stopped and noticed the time and shared my prayer with my sister, but I did. The next morning, Maggie called my cell. Knowing Maggie and how late she slept, I let the phone ring. Then it dawned on me that this was so out of character for her that I needed to call immediately. As I dialed the number, the voice mail appeared, and I heard these wails of crying, and I couldn't dial the numbers fast enough to get to my friend.

When the phone was answered, it was by her daughter, and she said, "Mom died last night in a car wreck." Maggie and her grandson and his other grandmother had rolled over after a truck pulled out in front of them. Everyone was okay but Maggie. I asked, "What time did this happen?" She informed me it was at 9:23 pm. She said, "Mom went through the windshield and was alive when the paramedics got there. They told her to wiggle her feet, and she wiggled her big toe, and then she died." My heart stopped. I sank to the floor, and I cried as if someone had taken the very air out of my lungs for the next few moments.

After that flight that day and the humiliation, Maggie never wore a seatbelt again. In the end, because she wasn't wearing a seatbelt, she was ejected through the front windshield of the car and died.

She entered my life when I was a RN and left my life when I was a writer. She also had entered my life during the first year of my marriage and left within a few days of its ending. Maggie had always told me she would never live to be fifty, and she didn't. She died a young, vibrant, beautiful woman. Even with everything I was going through with a child having a fifty percent chance of dying, with a divorce after twenty-one years together, it was Maggie dying that I was not prepared for at that time. I had given my divorce to God and asked forgiveness; I had given my child to God to take if it was his will, but I had no preparation for the loss of a best friend. At this very moment, I cry over the destruction one person's cruelty had on my friend's life. If you don't think your words hold power, ask someone who harbors anger at you. It will be because of words spoken or words not spoken, which is just as powerful.

I smile today because it wasn't Maggie in that helicopter that night, but it was around the same time. God gave me that prayer and the knowledge that someone was seriously hurt. I just didn't know it would be Maggie's family, friends, daughters, and grandchildren.

I so miss my friend, but each time I see a bumblebee, I smile and talk to Maggie.

As God grants me grace to help others, then I shall always be careful with each word I use. I am thankful God grants me wisdom, the ability to see things as they unfold, and the best friends I still cherish today.

God is so amazing with his love, and if you have learned anything from this story, pick up the phone and call a friend and tell them that you love them. Dissolve any anger against you. Never leave anyone without saying "I love you." Those were the last words that Maggie spoke to me the time I last called her. She said, "I can't talk right now, but I love you."

What a message to leave for those in your life!

Chapter 11:

The Green Mile

D o any movies or songs remind you of things that have happened in your life? Well, I can answer that for us all. The answer is yes. I was travel nursing and working in this extremely busy ER. During my off time, I often watched television. One night as I was searching the guide, I noticed the movie *The Green Mile*. When it came out in 1999, it made a huge impact on many people. Michael Clark Duncan played an inmate who was wrongly accused of murder and was on death row. Tom Hanks was a prison guard, and he was a fair and just man in this movie.

When we are around people that society labels as scum, trash, or beneath others, we can become numb and fail to see the good in situations. Working ER, sadly, every coworker and I have had this opinion at some time in our career-not often, but a few times. You label people. If you are a wise person, God always seems to show you just how wrong you are, and how unfair it is to judge people like that. Treat all with kindness, and above all, showing love is usually the lesson that keeps me grounded.

A few days after watching this movie again for about the fifth time, I strut into the ER, almost dreading my day. I gladly thank God for the ability to work and for helping me through the day, because it is a grueling job. In the state that I was working in at that time, there were several prisons, and inmates were often brought in to the hospital. I saw the stillness and numbness of many of the guards. Since I have been given grace, I go out of my way to treat patients who are inmates with respect and kindness.

I took my room assignment, and I have this black man who is around sixty. He is in restraints because he has the ability to harm himself and others. Sedating him took six men. He was around six foot six and weighed at least three hundred pounds. His voice was loud and actually really scary. You could hear the anger and feel the danger. When you are alone with him in a four-by-five-foot room, danger is present.

Since I am small, someone of this size can intimidate me very easily, especially when there is a guard from the hospital sitting outside his door for protection. Even though he was in restraints, sedated, and there was a guard present, no one wanted this guy for a patient, but I got him.

I walked in to assess him, and his voice literally made me silently ask God to protect me, and this peace engulfed me. I left the room after my assessment and said, "Thank you Lord." It was an ongoing battle with this man all day. He was ranting and raving, and everyone was like, "He is your patient, do something." I am like, "Really?" So, I just do what comes naturally, which was to find the story of his life. I began to read his history of problems. He had only been out of prison less than a year, for which he had served over forty years for murder. I think of the movie that I had watched and the lesson that I needed to learn from it.

This man's name was Hayden. It was possible that he had been convicted at a time when there was still massive discrimination. Who am I to know if he was guilty or innocent? That was not my battle because everyone else had judged him. Society had labeled him; and the government had convicted him; however, he did his time, so why does anyone have the right to judge him now?

So with this information in hand, I went into his room. I sat on the side of his bed. This is forbidden with a man like this, but I had grace with the help of God. I held his hand; again this is forbidden, especially with someone from prison, because of the incidence of AIDS and again, especially without gloves. My hand is bare and I have no fear. I spoke to him and told him who I am, where I am from, and about God and grace. I made my voice soft, as if I were speaking to a child, for God had informed me that he needed a mother. The words that I spoke, I had no idea from where they came or why they came out of my mouth. He looked up at me, and for a moment, his eyes smiled. His eyes glowed with greatness, as if you were telling a child Santa is coming tonight. Then tears rolled to the corners of his eyes and slowly slid to his cheeks and then onto my hands. When the first one dropped, I knew his despair.

This man had basically been raised in a prison. He was frightened in this place. He was tied to a bed and being injected with needles. Afterward he had the feeling of euphoria from the drugs. When he awoke, it all started again. How dare anyone not know what this man was feeling? What was his life in prison like? How much emotional damage was done to his mind? Whether he brought it upon himself or not, in my eyes he was still a frightened child who had no one. No one in the ER wanted him as a patient. No security guard wanted to sit outside his room, and no facility was available to transport him to. I cringe as I even begin to try and validate anyone's reasoning for this man.

I continued to go in and out of his room throughout the day, and each time I walked out, I smiled and said, "I love you, Hayden." He responded with, "I love you, too," and then he fell asleep in a peaceful state. My day turned out to be a great day, and I must admit I am grateful that Hayden showed me the lessons we all need each and every day. We must without a doubt, tell someone that they are loved. We must show humility to everyone, just as

Jesus did in his walk on earth. We must not be so willing to judge and label those that society could care less about.

At the end of my twelve-hour shift, Hayden was the last one I saw. As I exited his room I said, "I love you, Hayden," to which he replied, "I love you too, Momma." Tears then rolled down my cheeks.

The young security guy outside his door looked at me and asked, "Did you just tell him that you loved him"?

I said, "Yes."

He replied, "Did you not know that he killed someone? Why would you do that?"

Anger surfaced, then receded, and I answered, "I have no idea what that man has endured. I do not know his sin, nor is it my place to judge him when his debt has been paid. He deserves to know that someone walking on this earth loves him. I imagine that he only knew that through the eyes of his mother. I think he deserves to hear that." Then I looked at this young security guard and said, "I love you too." He did not reply.

See, all my life I have faced every form of discrimination known to a woman. I was discriminated against for being young and cute as well as young, obese, and ugly. I faced discrimination in jobs I held because I was a single mother with a young baby. The job I did get, I was paid less because I was a woman. First, I was discriminated against for being very obese, then again, for losing lots of weight later. It is just what our society does. They label people and get away with it. Being from the south with a thick southern accent, I was immediately labeled as a racist based on stereotypes.

I just never knew the discrimination of being black. I have to give Oprah Winfrey the credit for showing me that on one of her shows during Martin Luther King week few years back. I understood, but will never truly know its impact nor its injustice. I am thankful this is one thing that I will never experience. Then again, I am one of those people that doesn't have to go through things to understand and empathize.

God brings me through the hardships I face and teaches me the lessons that I need to learn. Over the years, I have learned that if I don't learn a lesson the first time, he will often give me a second chance to learn it. "I got you' God," I say then.

See, society labels our sins, our discriminations, our thoughts, our angers, and our injustices. It is based on what we listen to, what we read, and who we determine has worth. Also, it is based upon what we watch sitting on the sidelines of life. When we stay faithful in God's realm of love, we can't help but to make a difference to others. I can laugh with gladness at this statement now. Right when I think I am making a difference to someone else, God shows me it is they that have made the difference in my life.

My prayer for you today is to seek someone out that may be different from you. It could be someone your mind or society tells you that you are better than. Always say something honest, kind, and loving. God is love, and to walk in his grace, we must love all, not just those we think are in our social circles.

Chapter 12:

The Little Red Hen

Not long after my mother-in-law died, I took a job with the hospice company that was so good to her during her final days. I think one of the saddest days is when a patient is rolled into that home, because they will never leave there except in a body bag. Each breath of life they lived will be remembered inside the souls of those left behind. They will never feel the rays of warmth from the sun; they never again will inhale a crisp, cold winter day; and most will never see a bird outside the window as it lands on the feeder each day. To some, that will be the last sight that they will see before their soul is taken from earth. Prior to them coming in, I would see many at the nursing homes with dementia and other diseases that would stop the beating of their hearts someday. This was a new experience for me since I had only worked ER and ICU. I felt that God had placed me there for a reason. I will carry bittersweet memories of these patients for a lifetime, and I hope you pause and think of them when you are reminded of the story.

One of my first patients was a lady whom I shall call Elizabeth. I walked into her room, and there was this lady with a bold attitude—bossy, demanding, and could not care less if I were there or not. Let me say, first impressions are seldom right, and it took me many weeks to break through to see she was just like all women. She was laden with hopelessness, fear, brokenness and shame. She knew no difference. Her clothing was stained with snuff stains; she had a bib on, and still, the stains were ground into her clothes and to the side of her mouth, just like my grandmother Clara. I knew from Clara being in a nursing home, that this was a forbidden sin. It carried a cruel curse of judgment in the old days, just like smoking does today. Society gets to judge our sins, so like most people Clara's and Elizabeth's age, it was hidden the best way possible. It was still judged, but actually, only by herself and the shame that her daughter put upon her about her clothing. I still cringe at this shame that a child places on a parent at this stage in life. "We come into this world perfect; we should exit with the grace of exceptionalism," is what I write for these women of grace.

I had to visit Elizabeth three times a week. Often I would sit with her and talk, and after a few weeks I broke into the trust of her heart. Her room was filled with flowers and plants by the window, they were her joy. I recall the exact moment she found trust and love in me. She had a plant called "Hens and Chickens", which keep growing and coming back yearly. I had lost my own plant of this species years ago, and I just adored hers. I could easily afford to buy one, and had planned to do so one day when I had the time to care for it.

Elizabeth was watering this small plant and carefully cleaning its foliage, similar to the way an animal will clean its newborn after giving birth. As I watched, she snapped off a few of the roots and placed them in the napkin that she had used to wipe the snuff from her mouth. I smiled and gladly took this plant. I knew this was a gift beyond anything I could receive. I still think of that day and the words she said, "Please don't tell Emily (her daughter). Emily gave it to me." I thought sadly of how much pain this woman must have had and how much anger and pain this daughter carried as well. I took the plant and placed it carefully into my bag. I asked her why she liked this plant called "Hens and Chicks". She told me that her favorite childhood story was "The Little Red Hen."

My recollection of that book surfaced as well. It was a favorite of mine, too. I left and thought how blessed I was that day. I called a friend who told me that he would order that book for me, and I could pick it up. It was a three-dollar book, but to her, I knew that it would be a gift of memories past.

A few weeks later, I got the book and took it to Elizabeth's room. I was running late and thought I could just see her a moment. I would leave the book for her and her daughter to share. I think that I've really done a great job. I was so pressed for time, but I made it to her room. She was sitting there with a gleam in her eyes. She smiled as I entered. I explained that I was late but that I wanted to drop off the book. She says, "Will you read it to me?" I am thinking that I don't have time. I say my intent was to let her and her daughter share it together. She told me that Emily would never read it to her. I had tried my best to rush and get home early today. I asked her why she wouldn't read it for herself.

In that moment, I saw her eyes freeze in fear, her shoulders drooped. I looked at her, and God told me what was wrong. I said, "Ms. Elizabeth, can you read?" I knew the answer before I even asked the question. The tears that filled her eyes told me the answer. A tear dropped to her cheek, and a lump the size of an enlarged heart rose into my throat. I stopped; I sat down, and I read her the story. I began to cry, thinking of my own life and how often I had read to my son, and the priceless moments I was given.

Who was I to never take the time to stop and share this greatness of words and love? These are God's rewards for knowledge. Here I was upset with the daughter, yet I reacted similarly. That day was profound for me. I never again took a request for granted in that job. God always gave me peace with those about to leave this world. He cradled me with memories only I will carry at that age in life. He held me in the difficult times that I would have to surmount. In reading that childhood book to Elizabeth, it was I who was blessed, and I was getting paid for this blessing that had no price tag.

I shall not tell you the story of "The Little Red Hen" because it is a classic. It is a childhood memory, and it is a story for all ages. It contains a lesson that we all could use.

I laugh now and call myself "the little red hen." Believe me, I met a real one face to face. Although Elizabeth is deceased now, her handprint is forever branded on my soul, and she is part of who I am today.

Chapter 13:

Time

One morning as I was drinking coffee and watching a show, I begin to understand the little things in life that we take for granted, and it brought tears to my eyes. One of the most precious of those things is time. I remember as a child, Paul Harvey used to do a five-minute program called "The Rest of the Story." For some reason, I was always drawn to that part of the news nightly. It was when there were only four channels on a TV, and the news was nothing compared to today's coverage. In one of those segments, he said, "The greatest gift that we can give someone is our time." Jobs pay us for our time, which is why it is not taken as a waste. To give your time to help another is priceless. It still resonates with me, and in times in my life when I have given my time, I have found happiness. The sacrifice of my time is returned with laughter, love, and kindness worth more than any paycheck I could ever receive.

This show that I was watching this morning is a Missionary show. In this episode, they give a blind Jewish man a clock that speaks. It also allows him to read the time with his hands. I doubt that it costs very much in today's market. To that man, it was as if you had given him an amazing gift after a lifetime of not knowing the time. Think how many times in a day we look at a clock and take it for granted.

I remember sitting in a tiny apartment with my mother-in-law. Nothing was being said, and I heard this clock going tick, tock, almost to the point of annoyance. I glanced at her, and I thought, "Is this what I shall be doing when I get older?" I actually felt that I had to leave the room from the nausea I had gotten in the pit of my stomach. I asked if she would like to get out. Her answer was, "No." From that moment on, I went to see her as often as I could and did all that I could to help her. My reward was a love bound by no law of man, but from love.

Around eleven years after that time, I found myself in despair. I was going through a divorce; my best friend had been killed in a car accident; and my son was facing one of the biggest battles of his life with a chance of dying. I did not think I could handle much more emotionally. Often, when I am in despair and overwhelmed, I curl up in my bed. I ask God to hold me, hug me, and just show me how to make it through. Of course, I lay down and cried, and after about twenty minutes, everything was quiet. I heard the tick, tock of an inexpensive clock in my bedroom. I was reminded of that segment on TV from Paul Harvey. I remembered that day with Mary. Now my pity self and I knew that in the quietness of life, God gave me the answer. I jumped up out of bed like I was a little girl on Christmas morning, and I thanked God for answered prayers.

Jackson Brown has a quote that goes, "Don't say that you don't have enough time. You have exactly the same number of hours per day as given to Helen Keller, Pasteur, Michelangelo, Mother Theresa, Leonardo da Vinci, Thomas Jefferson, and Albert Einstein. We don't have to be important to have a purpose. We all are given gifts. Use your time wisely".

Chapter 14:

We Can't Take You

I often reflect back to my first days in nursing nineteen years ago and how consumed and awed I was with what was before me. I was a new nurse working night shift on the surgical floor. I remember taking a report, and as I listened to the words of the report being given, this feeling of sadness engulfed me. I knew that this lady was going to be my patient, and that she had no idea what was before her. Nor did I know what was before me. As I finished the report, I saved my visit to her room for last. I had the dread of not knowing the answers to the questions that I was going to be asked. It is a fear that grasps us daily. At this time, I did not have the grace or the faith that I do now. I couldn't even begin to comprehend the situation and its importance.

As I walked in, I noticed this tall, dark-haired man; a beautiful red-headed lady; and two children, a girl the age of around six and her brother of about eight. Having a son myself, I placed myself in her role as a mother, and I hugged both kids. The kids were edgy, so the husband took them downstairs to get something to eat while I stayed and spoke with Deanna.

She was thirty-two years old and has just been "feeling run down," as she put it. She proceeded to tell me that she had been very busy moving into a home because their home had burned down the month before. She thought it was just exhaustion, but was told the source of her problem after an MRI and an exploratory lap surgery. She was eaten up with cancer, and there was no hope. However, she had such faith and such grace and belief that it was all going to be better.

They were going to go to MD Anderson Cancer Research Center and had so many prayer warriors; she truly walked in faith. I just listened to her share how that the church had come together and gotten everything, including a home for them, after the fire. There was absolutely no doubt in her mind that she would be healed. I just stood there, young and at that time, not very knowledgeable about cancer. In the back of my mind I thought, "No way."

As the night grew into morning, and as I spent more time with her, I was just as convinced as she was that she would be healed. The next morning, as I left work, I went to see her. I explained that I was off for a few days and gave her a hug. A few weeks later, I came in and got a report, and of all people, I had Deanna as a patient again. I went to her room first this night, and as I walked in, I saw her in tears. Her husband was holding her as tightly as he could. I cannot even imagine what emotions, turmoil, or pain they were in at this time. As I approached, I asked about going out to the cancer center. She replied that they could not take her because the cancer had raped each viable cell within. It wasn't that they didn't want to help her, there just nothing they could do. I started to cry then, and I wondered why.

Then about six days later I opened the paper. Being a nurse, you always read the obituaries because it tells you more about your patient than you knew. Right before my eyes was Deanna's obituary. I remember asking God, "Why?" To this day I do not know why things like this happen. She crossed my journey not once, but twice. I smile as I write this story, thinking that she had a purpose in my journey, and how blessed I am to have been a part of hers. She did have a purpose and a place in my heart, and she still does today.

You know, as children we make molds of handprints when we are small, and for some reason, they last a lifetime. Well, Deanna is one of those handprints on my heart that will not break.

I guess, what I am trying to define, is how it must feel for someone to say, "We can't take you." This world could not take her, but God took her. The impact of her story should teach us all to rely on faith, and not man's word. Be bold and graceful, be blessed, and be thankful for each day that God grants us all. Never allow anyone to say, "We can't take you."

Chapter 15:

Locked In

As I relay these stories, I do not Google the medical term or the in-depth medical knowledge. I am explaining these things in the way that they were explained to me. I learned to experience the knowledge and relay it in simple terms.

I was fairly new to ICU and had just gotten my feet wet inside this intensive medical field. I came in on an evening shift and I had a patient that I always refer to as Randy. He reminded me of Randy Travis with his looks and his build. It was on this day that I learned two medical terms that I have never forgotten. Often, I told this story when I had to explain them to another.

Randy was in his mid-fifties, and from what I was told, he was at one time big in politics and was well-known. He and his ex-wife remained friends. From what little I had gathered, I imagine they were more than just friends, and maybe possibly on the way back together. She often came to his house during the week, and he went to hers. After several days of him not answering her calls, she decided to go and check on him. When she arrived, she found him soaked in urine, unable to speak, and with only his eyes showing signs of life. She called the paramedics, and he was transferred to the larger ICU that we had available. I had no idea the impact this day would make on my life. I still think of Randy and wonder if he still lives. Honestly, I don't think anyone would want this life based on the story that unfolds.

Randy had fallen after having a stroke. From there he developed rhabdomyolysis, which was explained to me as muscle wasting. When someone falls or lies in a place with no movement, like after a stroke, the muscle begins to break down and spill protein into the kidneys. It can be treated, but success depends upon the damage.

I went in to see Randy and to observe him for my charting. I talked to his sister, who was at his bedside. Actually, she spoke as if he was not there. His eyes were closed, and as I spoke, he opened them for me. Brightness beamed off the prettiest blue eyes that I had ever seen on a man. I always look at someone's eyes because I think that people's hearts show through their eyes and their smiles. Randy could not smile, but his eyes were smiling at me. I listened to the story his sister told, and then she asked me a few questions. To be honest, I had not looked at the chart. I did not know where his stroke was, or what the outcome would be. I saw the neurologist at a distance, and he knew that I am nurse of questions and eager to learn. He told me that Randy had a stroke in the region of the brain that, when it hit, it locked him in. He called it "locked-in syndrome." In other words, this was as good as it would ever get for Randy. He was locked into his own head, and his eyes would be the only part of him that moved. The doctor explained that his mind was present and he understood every word that was spoken, but he could not react.

I cannot begin to imagine what living like this would be for anyone. The damage was done, and life for Randy would be no more. Can you even begin to deal with that? Never being able to laugh to smile, to talk, to eat, or to hold someone that you love would be a very hard and cold existence. Can you at this moment imagine what that must feel like to someone like Randy? As the doctor explained, I began to cry and turned my head so that no one could tell. It's what we do to cope, but my coping is with this story. I have shed many tears in this collage of life, if for no other reason than to stop and be aware of how an instant can change our lives. Some days we can't repeat. Each person in these stories affected my life and now, hopefully, yours also.

I ended up with only Randy and one other patient that night. I spent lots of time with him after his sister left. I spoke quietly and carefully, and watched the reaction from his eyes when I asked a question. I told Randy that I could not imagine his grief. I explained to him that I understood if he didn't want to live. The awareness that I saw in his eyes from that statement, begged me to help him end his life. As sure as I write this story, I know that is what Randy wanted more than anything. Of course, my job is to save and not to take. Honestly, if that were me laying in that spot, I think I would want the same thing. You have to be careful with judging. I think people have the right to make a choice to end a life easily, and I think each should have the right to live. However, I am neither judge nor jury to decide that fate. I am only the messenger, and until you see both sides, you have no voice to speak for those that can't, like Randy.

The neurologist visited again that night. Knowing this doctor as well as I did, I considered him to be a friend. He was gruff, strong, and opinionated, but tonight his heart was heavy. I think he identified with Randy. He told me that Randy would most likely go to a nursing home and die. Sadly, there is no law to give him any other rights. His choice was made for him by being locked in. Even the doctor struggled with this and wished that he could help. Like me, I think Randy's story often comes to his mind. This doctor's son eventually took his own life. I don't know the story, or need to know. I saw a man broken that night. Maybe these situations contribute to us in the medical field being able to shut out others so that they don't see the pain that we do carry. I have no clue. I only know of my struggles and seeing life beyond the patient's name and diagnosis. I see the depth that God's grace has granted me.

As I left that night, I went to clock out. I came and sat at Randy's side and held his hand. I know the sensation of touch was not there, but his eyes told me that I had reached his heart. I wept as I started to go, as does Randy. I know I will never see him again because I am off for a week. I tell him that I will often think of him, and one day I hope to help others in this situation. All I can do is tell you a different side.

I don't think any of us need to make decisions for others based on our perceptions of the right thing. We should make them based on the wishes in the hearts of those we love. If it were you in this situation, may I ask what would your choice be? Hard choice, isn't it?

Chapter 16:

Lonely

I had a patient who came into the ER with chest pain. She was fifty-seven years old. She was a beautiful woman. As I sat down to start an IV on her, I took the opportunity to learn about her life. I saw this despair that only a woman alone at this age understands. Her children were grown. Her husband, whom she had adored, died six years ago. She had just lost her job and was going to have to go on Medicaid. You could tell it was killing her to use the system.

I sat down and spoke with her and asked why she chooses to be alone.

She said, "I don't."

I asked her if her husband and she had a good relationship. She smiled and said, "Yes."

"Did he love you?"

She said "Yes," again.

I said, "Ok, so you are in a bad spot."

I told her about my son, who was $300,000 in debt from hospital bills and who, for the first time in his life, had to ask for charity. Then I explained that it was ok. It is there to be used by those in need. Because we don't agree with the system, and how it is abused, we find ourselves feeling guilty over using it when we need it. From the expression that she displayed, I knew that's what she felt. I also explained that if her husband had loved her, he would not want to see her dealing with this alone. She agreed.

I also told her that we are truly never alone. God is always there, and if you want someone to share your life with then you learn about faith. You learn about guilt and how it bolts the joy out of you. I told her to believe that life is a journey not meant to be spent alone. Until she knew that she is loved by God, and learned to love herself, then no one worthy of her would be placed into her life.

We continued to talk, and I told her how beautiful she was, how kind she was, how worthy she was, and only by grace from God was I allowed such knowledge. By the end of the treatment, I told her that I loved her, and she smiled and said, "I love you too, and thank you."

We all have gifts to share and explore with others. It just takes a bit of time to stop and see others. It is only through the grace of God and women like her, that we see ourselves, and where we too, once were in our life. My prayer today is that you tell someone something good about them. Ask God to continue to bless you with words and grace to make a difference. And thank you, God, for reminding us that without your love, we would never know grace or the experiences it brings to us.

Chapter 17:

Mere Seconds

How often do we take things for granted? Tomorrow is not promised us, and yet we live as if each day is going to come. The ambulance brought in a fifty year old male, and just from the compressions they were doing and the color of his skin and the stillness of anything except the reaction one would have from CPR being done on a human, you could tell that this was this man's last day on earth. I was extremely busy, and he was not my patient, but I had to go and find out his story, and its purpose and meaning.

This man had gotten up on a Sunday morning and gone outside in the snow to play with his young children. When the children came in from outside, their mom asked, "Where is your dad?"

The nine-year-old replied, "He fell asleep in the snow."

Little did this child know that this day would forever be branded in her mind. She will carry extreme feelings from this day with a misunderstanding that she had done something wrong. If her family or someone in her life can help her to understand this, it will be very beneficial to her. Isn't it strange how life changes in mere seconds and affects the course of so many others? Do you know a child like this? Do you know a wife like this? If you do, and you are of grace, then make a difference! We have no idea the power that we have to help someone in need. We have no idea why, or how God can use us, unless we ask. If one person makes a difference, isn't it worth it? It only takes a few words, a hug, an understanding and the grace of God to help those with life-changing moments.

My prayer is, "God please teach me to be a better friend to those that seek you. Help me to help those who are unable to help themselves. God, I ask your divine power to watch over each child that we can help, and help us all to be thankful for the mere seconds that we have to make a difference."

Chapter 18:

Artificial Lights

I recall a bright, sunny day when I was working inside the ICU. I did not want to be there on such a day, but like most that work, we don't get to choose our workdays. We also don't get to choose many other split-second things that happen to change the course of our lives.

I was working with two patients, and both were on ventilators. It was a hard day physically, having to turn patients. I had to ask for help every two hours. It was also emotionally draining. If at any time that machine beeps and you don't address the problem, you are shouldering the responsibility that the patient could die without this machine. It is very demanding.

The ICU is contained inside, with a cubicle with two windows where you are always watching both patients and charting. If at any time you leave, someone has to be notified that you are leaving. When you are searching for someone to help you turn the patients, it is extremely hard because of the isolation of this cubicle.

I was tired, ready to go home, and about to do my last turn of a twelve-hour shift when I searched for help. I was frustrated because I could not find anyone to help me. I heard some voices across from where my patients were. I walked into a room where four people were helping a nurse. Looking at the patient, he was a man of around six feet tall, strong, and quite handsome, if you saw him in a different environment than today. However, today he was fragile. He was fearful, and I noticed sorrow in the expression on his face. His bed was in "stand" position to assist with turning him. He was on a ventilator, and his skin tone was ghostly pale in appearance, like Casper the cartoon character.

I noticed that his hands were not tied down, which was unusual because ICU patients on a ventilator often react when awakened. You can imagine, with a tube the size of a small water hose crammed into your lungs, and you wake up alone with artificial lights above, it can cause a reaction from fear. You have no idea what is going on around you. It is a normal reaction, and most are sedated until their lungs have the capacity to expand on their own. Even with sedation, many still react with fear and attempt to pull out their tube. This is why we often place ventilator patients in restraints to protect them. There is nothing scarier than a patient taking out the endotracheal, which is providing them with needed oxygen. It is a trauma that can, and is avoided inside these artificial settings.

She informed me that he had AIDS. At this time, it was one of the worst labels to have, and the worse disease to have. However, as I heard the rest of the story, it was nothing compared to his label of life that he had left. She explained that he had only been diagnosed with AIDS for less than a year, and a few nights ago, he was sitting on his deck having wine. I imagined that he was thinking, like most with this disease would, about the process his body was about to undertake. I can only imagine that he was confused and asking God why and asking himself why, and trying to understand this new disease that had surfaced internationally and harbored such judgment from many.

Honestly, I can imagine what he is asking himself. I can relate to this because, as a new nurse, within the first years, I got stuck with needles and had to take tests to see if I had HIV and hepatitis. I often thought, "What if

I was positive? I wouldn't live to see my son grow up; I would not get to hold my friend's new baby; my family and friends may isolate me." I wondered how to handle this responsibility, this fear, and this judgment.

Rampant thoughts consumed me with 'what if.' I could imagine his questions, his reasoning, and his idea of what others would think. I can say, that it is a lonely, fearful existence. It stems completely from the judgment of society during this time.

To understand the stigmatism, you must remember that this was in the era before Magic Johnson showed us another picture of its ravage. Whether it was HIV or AIDS, people are brutal. Ryan White's life showed me that many years prior to being a nurse. As Payne stood to get up, and as he came around the chair on his deck, his cat Abbey had rubbed against his feet. Cats do this because they release pheromones that make them feel safe. As Abbey found her safe place and rubbed against him, Payne tripped. From there he tumbled down the deck stairs, and life as he thought was over became unbearable. Luckily, Payne had a friend inside his home that heard this fall and called 911. As Payne was rolled into his room that night, I am sure those questions he asked thirty-six hours previous of 'what if' no longer had worry. Payne's worry and grief was that never again would he enjoy the tartness of Merlot; the serenity of sitting outside on his deck; and feeling Abbey's reaction to safety against his feet. He now was paralyzed; he had full-blown AIDS; and now his last days wouldn't be at home with family and friends surrounding him. His family had shunned him when he came out of the closet. It is sad how that phrase 'coming out of the closet' actually places you in a closet based on others' judgment. Should we really shun anyone with sin or our label of sin?

I remember going home that night with such sorrow. Here I was complaining of working on a pretty day. I complained because of the turns I had to make. All day this thirty-two-year-old man was less than ten feet from the cubicle where I had spent my day thinking only of myself. What right did I have to feel anything but love, thankfulness, gratefulness, and humbleness for every label in society? I can walk; I can sit on my deck and have Merlot; I can hug someone; I can be kind; and most of all, I can choose not to judge anyone's sins. I can choose not to judge anyone by the label that society gives them. I can always look for someone to help me with my turns, but with Payne's story, I learned to always look around, to see the whole picture. If I feel sorry for myself, tired of working, sad that I'm inside for a day, I can always remember others have it far worse than me.

I recently had a stray cat come up, and I was reminded of Payne. I harbored such dislike for cats after that day, but I smiled, I watched my steps, and I allowed my Abbey to feel safe. Yes, I named her Abbey, for the few weeks she was here. Now I understand that God sends me the stories that he wants you to hear.

Do not judge, be thankful, be humble, be loving, and if you come across someone in life that society has labeled, make them feel safe. It is what Jesus would do. How simple it is that kind words, a smile, and a gesture of grace can bring joy to others.

Chapter 19:

Aha Moments

When I first began nursing, one of the "aha" moments I had was with a small boy. I had completed my rounds, and looking back now, I can always remember that I wanted to hear people's stories. I had childlike curiosity, and the boldness to ask, and the empathy to bear the pain that most must feel. I remember it was a bright, sunny day, but I was inside the walls of a hospital ward where most of the lights are artificial. At the end of each hall was a window. I often would go there to see the sun and feel the warmth of its rays. Most patients' rooms had windows that were often closed and there was seldom anything but the artificial light available.

One day I was ahead on rounds and decided to go to the window to see what was going on outside. I wanted to see who was taking the time to enjoy the sunny day outside. As I rounded the corner, I saw the rays of the sun reflect on the floors. As I glanced up, I saw a child around nine year's old standing in the spot where I often stood to look outside the walls of the hospital.

I stopped in my tracks and noticed this child, who was close to the age of my son. He was tall, thin, and his color was pale, even though he was of African descent. I walked up to him and saw his name on the wristband that was needed to be admitted into the hospital. I tell him that I have a son close to his age and that each week he calls someone to come and pick him up at school, because he is sick. My son is seldom sick once he gets inside the love of a grandmother's home after that call. I explain that to this child, Josh, and smile. Josh returns it with a smile that naturally shows great pain. I looked at Josh, and I said, "You would give anything to go to school today, wouldn't you?" He turned his head away because he knew I had identified his thoughts. I asked Josh why he was in the hospital, and this child began to tell me of his struggle.

Josh was diagnosed with sickle-cell anemia. Often when a crisis with this disease hits, he has to be hospitalized for the severity of the pain. From what little I knew of the disease, I asked him what that pain was like. He explained how that it felt as if his legs and arms are being squeezed to the point of excruciating pain. He often wished that he didn't have the limbs. He was a child, and he had no idea the impact of having no limbs would bring. Being an adult, I understood that he didn't mean it literally. In his childlike manner, with the voice of a young man ahead of his age, he had spoken those words. My heart poured sorrow for his pain.

I can best describe sickle cell crisis in a simple form that I had remembered from listening to and reading about it that day. Our blood cells are round, and in a sickle cell crisis they become oblong. Because our vessels are formed to fit round cells, oblong cells have to be forced into a vessel that they don't fit into. It's like having a round dining table and placing an oblong tablecloth on it. It doesn't fit, yet it still works if we have to have it.

Josh and I spoke and I learned that he couldn't play sports. He missed school often, and he didn't fit in with his peers. Because of my childhood, I understood this child's pain. I didn't know then what I know now, but this disease would cause him pain as a child. In the core of my soul, I knew that this child will make a difference in life from his pain.

See, I thought I was going to be a good person, nurse, or mom-like figure to Josh. For some reason, we often are drawn to the light most of the time to help ourselves. Despite the age difference, and the place in life that Josh and I were on that day, we were on equal ground and were friends for a day. God made our skin color different and our perceptions of life different. No matter how grown up we are, children teach us so much about life. Josh taught me the pain of a patient in crisis. I would reflect on that child with a young man's voice that said it hurts. When I got the opportunity to be blessed with a sickle cell patient, or when a peer received one, I often told the story of that day with Josh.

When I returned home that day, I hugged my son so hard that I am sure he felt the tightness squeezed from his limbs. I informed him of the day with Josh and how he was often sick and couldn't go to school, play sports or be hugged as tightly as I had just hugged my son. It never stopped my son from calling home sick from school, and looking back now, he didn't have the experience of Josh's pain and life. His pain came from within the core of his soul. Being loved by a grandmother helped him alleviate the pain of the life going on inside his walls of school. To be honest, that epiphany hits me today. I realize what I wasn't seeing inside my own life then, but I am grateful for it today.

I am thankful to have fears and challenges. For without them, we couldn't identify or understand how great our strengths are to others. Without the grace of God and the pain I endured in childhood, never would I have stopped to see the stories of others contained inside the collage of my life.

Chapter 20:

Acknowledging the Overlooked

How many times do we forget and overlook people we think are not worthy of our time? Have you thought about those people and the difference they make in our lives? Working in an ER is fast paced, and by that I mean, we are tearing open IV sets, oxygen sets, and throwing things on the floor just to save a life. Sometimes we do it for the non-critical as well. We still leave things on the floor because we know that housekeeping is going to clean it up fast for the next person in line. Shamefully, I must admit that I too, have done this. One day I was cold and this lady who weighed no more than 100 pounds saw my coldness and went to surgery to get me a gown to wear to keep warm. I tell you, at that moment, I asked her to forgive me for leaving the messes that I had left for her to clean up. She smiled sweetly and said that it was ok. From that moment on, I heard the most amazing stories about housekeeping.

There was a guy named Michael, who was quiet, and he did his job well. One night we were slow, and I thanked him for cleaning up one of my rooms. I sat with him and asked him about his life. This man, who was in his late fifties or early sixties, told me that he had been married for about forty-five years. He had a daughter in the nursing home who was twenty-eight years old. She had been in a car wreck in her teens from drinking and driving. She was basically brain dead. He had another daughter who was about to give birth to his first grandchild. I listened as his eyes lit up with delight speaking of his family. I saw his shoulders slump when he spoke of his daughter who threw away her life with a bad choice. I saw the vast amount of strength this man had with peace inside.

This man was a janitor, and his purpose was much greater than mine. All he did was go around and clean up everyone's mess. He never complained, was never angry, and was always gentle, quiet, and kind. When I would ask him things later, I noticed that the staff did not know much about this man. I thought, lucky me, to know such a man. How dare any of us think, because we have a degree because we make more money, or because our social status is a bit above others, how dare we think that those who clean up after everyone else are of no value? See, Michael saw his own value. He saw the pride of walking into a room that he had just cleaned, and he never once complained. Isn't Jesus like this? Doesn't he want us all to stop, notice, and value the people we think are below average? Who are we to ever think that at any point in our lives? How does one say they are Christian and not love the housekeepers, the janitors, the nurses, and think only of those of a higher social standing are better?

God is love, and Jesus is love, and that means we must love, respect, and appreciate all his creations. Not just the ones we think are worthy. We are not the judges, and if we think we are, our duty as Christians becomes a negative behavior that others judge Christians by.

My prayer today is, "God forgive me for the messes that I have left. Thank you for the ones you have cleaned up, and I ask you to help everyone to see their value through your love and your devotion to us. May we all be beacons of light in Jesus's name. Father, forgive me, and thank you for showing me who helps me on a daily basis, from housekeeping, to janitors, to those in the medical professions. Thank you God, for giving us the privilege to know such people in our lives."

Chapter 21

The Gift of Life

End of life issues and decisions I believe are one of the hardest things a family must do. Many times in life I would think to myself, could I do such as that I asked of others?

It wasn't until my aunt called me one day and asked me to help her make the right decision. My grandmother who was bed bound, no quality of life and also in her 90's and was placed on the DNR (Do not resuscitate) list. DNR is when one allows the natural dying process to move forward with no interventions. Having such responsibility on any family no matter the age or the quality of life left, it still surrounds hurt in my thoughts of how hard something like this is on a family. See if I needed to learn something seems God always showed me the little things that are huge in the life of others by allowing me to experience myself. We as medical professionals think we know the answers, yet once faced with these issues, reality and love bring us full throttle to memories past when we also have to make decisions to allow such process. It is a burden one shouldn't have to make; however, in today's world someone has to do it and carry that burden. As time passes that burden is lifted but only by the grace of God and family left. It is with such experience I write the story of Phillip.

I was working in ICU (Intensive Care Unit) and my patient that day was Phillip. Phillip had arrived the previous night from the Air Vac which had airlifted him to this unit from a MVA (motor vehicle accident) Phillip was around 19 years old, locks of blonde hair, around 5'9 and thin. Based upon the sculpture of his physique I would say he may could bench press a lot more than my own son could at this stage in his life. I say this because my son was younger and beginning to learn the importance of how physical appearances were judged by his peers. He was working out, drinking the shakes that promote such appearance and only because of him, I understood somewhat of weight lifting and its rewards.

Phillip like many in the early innocence of teenage years forwarding toward adulthood and believing he was wise beyond his years had gotten behind the wheel of his truck, fast and furiously driving and lost control and flipped his truck. Based on his injuries I could tell it had to have been at a high speed with ejection from the back windows of the late model truck he was driving. I know this because most of my day was spent keeping him alive on multiple iv drips, a ventilator forcing his lungs to expand with oxygen being forced to capacity to survive and based upon the ventilator settings reminds me he is not breathing any on his own. During times I continued to clean these locks of blonde hair while pulling pieces of glass out of his toned muscles, his skull and his arms. I'll never forget thinking I understood the concept of when glass breaks; it breaks into millions of pieces; I lost count of how many pieces I pulled out that day, but not without the reminder that this was someone's son, and silently I thanked God it wasn't my son. Strange how once motherhood is bonded within our wombs each child we see or hear of like Phillip we thank God it isn't our child, and immediately empathy and love is all we have to offer other parents. It is a natural instinct, reaction and understanding how easily this could be your child. Let me remind each of you it can and will happen to someone you know during your lifetime.

After I had finished trying to clean the fragments of glass, wash and comb the curly locks it was time for family to visit. Phillips mom and dad with a few more members came inside the cubicle of ICU. His mom looked at her son, then looked to the monitors, the ventilator and then me. I froze. Earlier when the doctor had made rounds and we talked, I remember asking him "Is this chart right? Is he brain dead?" See fear of the unknown use to frighten me beyond anything I can write. Fear of losing a child frightened me when it visited my dreams after caring for anyone's child. It was a reason I never worked with pediatrics, and each of us should be thankful for nurses willing to take on such, for sure, it isn't me, yet after a child turns 18 they are considered adults and ICU is where they are placed.

Phillip's mom, Anna, looked at me for hope, she looked to me to help and I believe she was looking inside my eyes to see if my heart understood. It is for this reason I froze. She begins to cry as she touches her son; I step back in the corner for this is a day I can't bring sunshine of hope to them. I can only be the darkest cloud of kindness and answers experience has taught me. As I watch Anna I think of my own son and I weep. Not like Anna, for I have my son and I know the moment I get to see his face, inhale his scent and hold him in my arms will be the best part of my day today. It is for Phillip's family I weep.

Phillip's parents are not willing to let him go just yet as they are praying for a miracle, A miracle did happen but not in the way a parent would wish for.

For several weeks I had Phillip on and off. Anna brought cartoons of Power rangers, music Phillip loved and cards of hope and love were pasted upon the walls that showed no resemblance of an ICU unit but more of a child /teenagers room.

Each day I worked, if I had Phillip as a patient or not I always checked on him and his family. I began to look forward to going to work to see if any progression had transpired. Often on days I was off I would call and check on him with the same answer "there is no change." but like Anna I had faith even knowing it would be the greatest of miracles to witness.

After being off for several days I was assigned Phillip. I was informed instead of having two patients I was assigned to have only one and it would be Phillip per family request. I looked at the charge nurse and said why just one patient? She replied, "The fluids he was being given were not maintaining his blood pressure, he is crashing and the family had to decided donate his organs. This process was called "harvest organs". Let me just say it is a day I shall never forget in life. When organs are donated, even back years ago, the patient is taken to surgery while his organs are removed. My job for the day was to keep him alive until transplant teams arrived, and surgery could be done for these procedures. If you can comprehend stress of knowing this one patient will save so many lives and my role was to keep him alive to save others. It doesn't sound like something one would want but the benefits of saving so many is a gift I forever appreciated. To be given the gift of life from someone's death I believe is a priceless gift to others.

That afternoon as the surgery team wheeled Phillip out of the ICU I began to cry. For a brief moment I hated this job. I got tired of seeing destruction of death, pain of losing one so loved and one whose age makes me question why?

God gave his son for all to have eternal life. Anna gave her son for seven others to have life on earth. It is only grace that understands this gift and if anything I could ask of each of you is to accept Jesus as your savior. One other thing is to ask all to become a donor. We never know when we may be on the waiting list of life.

Dedication and Mom's Letter from Heaven

Maybe that was the intent, to make each and every one of us stop and realize that we don't have to be famous to be noticed. I guess God gave me a gift to be able to see these stories of pain and to become a better person through my job. He gave me a book to show others that when you come into the life of a medical person or situation, sometimes your story will stay branded on their hearts. When we try to help others, in truth we are helping ourselves.

We are not heroes; we do not seek favor; we are humans. I often watch YouTube videos of people who never stop and notice someone on the streets. The other day, I watched a video that was set up to see how many people would help a homeless man with one leg and on crutches as he falls. I cried thinking, "How did this world get to such a point?" It brings me to scriptures we all need to read. Matthew 25:35-40

"For I was hungry and you gave me food, I was thirsty and you gave me drink, I was a stranger and you welcomed me, I was naked and you clothed me, I was sick and you visited me, I was in prison and you came to me."

Then the righteous will answer him, saying, "Lord, when did we see you hungry and feed you, or thirsty and give you drink? And when did we see you a stranger and welcome you, or naked and clothe you? And when did we see you sick or in prison and visit you?"

And the King will answer them, "Truly, I say to you, as you did it to one of the least of these my brothers, you did it to me."

See, God gives us the tools that we need in life. If our hearts truly walk in love, we shouldn't have to be reminded of such trivial philosophy, but sometimes we do. If this book helps but one person to do so, then my purpose has been fulfilled.

The names of everyone in this book have been changed. Most of the details are from my memory. It was only after I lost a really good friend that I began to recall these stories. I went deep into the hurt of losing her; losing a marriage; and almost losing my only child. See, readers, I too, am not perfect and have a long way to go. I can say, had it not been for the grace of God and some very good and loyal family and friends, I don't think I could have made this journey. I am so fortunate to have them now.

I think we all have two sets of eyes, which I call spirit eyes and earthly eyes. I think God gave me the ability to see through both at the same time during these stories.

These situations are real; they happen to someone each and every day. We need to get up, starting on our knees daily to remind us all life changes in a split second. Any one of these people could have been you or a family member. I tell you again, when you go home each day after a traumatic shift, it doesn't end for some of us. Granted, it doesn't happen every day to affect our lives, but the ones that do, linger your whole life. We as nurses have sat around and brought up stories from years past and said, "Do you remember that girl that they said was going to die? I wonder what happened to her." See, even when we don't know how things turn out, they stay with us.

If you ever have smelled cancer as it has surfaced externally, it is a smell that is indescribable. Once, I left a patient in ICU that died as my shift ended.

Dedication and Mom's Letter from Heaven

The smell of cancers' rage permeated the whole ICU. I got inside my car with that smell still inside my nostrils. I went to a ballgame, and as I walked up to my friend, she said, "What is that smell?" Even in an open field, with cologne misted on my clothes trying to mask the odor, that odor took life within the particles of air and radiated the smell of cancer. I loathe that smell and rarely smell it, but one whiff, and I know it is around me. It is one reason that we use vapor rub in order to not inhale its rage.

When you have walked inside your home and see a drop of blood on your shoe, one drop, knowing that it was someone's last drop they shall shed, you cry. That drop of blood was an ending to a life that someone loved, and you toss it into the washer to erase its trace. When you have heard the scream of a mother losing a child, trust me, even the movies can't mimic its sound. The sounds of a heart breaking can only be felt. If you are a parent, you can only imagine if you have not lived this sound. No movie, no person, nor any situation can understand its meaning. It is a moment that you don't want to be in the middle of.

After a days' work, sleep is granted as a reprieve from the emotional and physical demands of these days. Even the alarm clock takes on a hospitals' presence. I truly have gotten up with darkness surrounding me, and I think, "Oh no! It's a ventilator or an IV pump going off." Fear engulfed me until I woke up to reality and realized it was just the alarm clock. I smiled, it was set to wake up my child to begin his day. I got up and I went to find the most loving thing God has granted us, the innocence of a child. I smiled, thanked God, and started my day. Even though I was off work, my heart reminded me of an event. I got my coffee and began to read the newspaper and the first pages that I always go to are the obituaries. I monitor the last days of someone whose hands you held. This is a day I hadn't clocked in for payment, yet still it remains within my own hearts' time clock. I think this book is needed to remind us or to inform so many people that we as nurses, doctors, and medical workers give so much to our jobs.

I am blessed to have worked in areas and during a time when nursing meant something. There was time to make a difference. These nurses and doctors and medical workers today are treated with so much disrespect. Sadly, now society, management, and government has said, "If you don't be nice, the hospital loses funding." So much stress is placed on us that this is a dying profession. We have to correct it one day at a time, one person at a time, and love each person that comes within our own personal space. I think I will write a book on the abuse that comes inside the ERs and how it continues to happen. People outside this system would be horrified to know how abused it is today. But I have to say that on many days, I still receive blessings, and some days the patients take my hand and they listen to my hurt. It is on those days, I know that God sends these patients to me at just the right time.

I cannot end this chapter or this book without saying a thank you to Gods' grace; to my best friend who spent countless hours helping me and believing in me when I could go no further; and to my dad for giving me a foundation of Gods' abundance of love. I thank my dad for his faith, with which he surrounded me daily. I also thank my son. Without him I don't know if my heart could have loved this much. As much as I love these people in my life, the greatest thing that I have is being called a child of God, for without his mercy, forgiveness, and love nothing would be possible.

I plan to follow with a book called "Journey Shoes", which is the story of my life. Each story listed above will help you to understand why God places us inside the lives of those he calls children. I am not famous, nor do I hold various degrees. I am just like you. I am human. I am a woman who makes mistakes, a woman who tries to be the best I can be, and a woman who wants to make a difference to those I meet each day. I strive for that daily, and I may not obtain it, but it shall not be from lack of trying.

Last, let me say this to those inside the chapters of the book, "Your life mattered, as does everyone's." We all matter to someone, so let's begin each day by reminding others. Do a kind deed, say a kind word, or pick up the phone and call a friend that God lays upon your heart. Just do it; kindness is contagious; and you might just find you get back more than you give.

Two years after writing this book my son died. I honor God for bringing such an abundance of love, empathy and humbleness. As you read this book, if you don't believe there is a God, this book was written before his death. It radiates within each chapter. After his death I was crying to a friend. I stated, "I have nothing left to lose," he stated back," You had better think about that." I humbly got down on my knees, I shouted to God, "Thank you for my health, thank you for my friends and just thank you Lord for accepting me as I am; protecting me; and giving me the faith to get up and do that which you have asked of me. I thank you Jesus!

So, as I began to move forward again in life, this letter from heaven arrived in my heart. To honor my son, I share this letter so that others will know that your child, like most in these stories, is in the palms of the greatest man that walked this earth. His name is Jesus, and without a doubt, our children are safer than any of us today reading this collage of life.

Mom's Letter from Heaven

Dear Mom,

I know that you can't see me, hear me, touch me or feel me, except in your heart, so let me began by saying, "I'm doing better in heaven beyond what anyone knows of heaven. I've asked God to send you signs of this peace through the little things that you always tried to get me to see as your child. I know you have lost your smile, and Mom, others that loved me too, need your smile back. God sees how clouded your mind has been. He understands each tear that you have shed, and He asked that you come to him as these tears begin, and let him hold you."

Mom, I am fine and without a doubt, I want you to understand that I have never been happier than or as peaceful as I am since arriving here. I understand the hurt that you will carry from my absence on earth, yet I also know how amazing God is by allowing me to come home.

Mom, I love you, I can't lessen your hurt, but I can validate that everything you told me about Jesus is true. You know Mom, God gave his son so that I may have this peace, so when you cry, follow those tears with smiles. One day we both will be inside this grace of heavens' pleasures together. Mom, I wish that you would wish upon the stars again like you taught me. I want you to dance in the rain like you did with me. See Mom, I need you to let me go. Place me in the memory box of love, place me inside the soul windows of your heart, and open these as you let me go.

Mom, I know that if wishes came true, you would want me to be there, however, that is not to be, and the reasons are not clear yet. One day it will be clearer, or at least somewhat bearable. You always told me that when I got older, I would understand things, now I'm asking that of you.

I must go now Mom. Jesus is calling, and like you once said, "He comes first." Just know that our Heavenly Father sees your pain and wants you to finish his calling for you on earth first. He has promised you in his word that there are three great things in life: faith, hope and love. Right now, you are mourning the greater of these things, which is love. To continue, you must now have faith and hope to grant you comfort. God has promised each of those that believe a place in heaven, and Mom, He's taken me in and He has a place for you too!

I'm hoping to receive my angel wings soon, then maybe I, too, can help others.

I've got to go now Mom.

I love you.

I love you too, my son. You were the best thing that ever happened to me.

God bless, Cera
Cera Grace LLC